About the book

Here is a book Federal Government bureaucrats will loathe. And it is a book that will delight ordinary citizens of all ages who have struggled with a Big Brother bureaucracy determined to have its way over all the little brothers and sisters it is supposed to serve.

Storm is about one man, Irving Krick, and the Federal establishment responsible for forecasting the nation's weather. While everyone talks about the weather, Krick has been doing something about it. This has displeased the Federal establishment that—whatever its current name—is known to ordinary folk as the Weather Bureau.

Krick is a professional meteorologist who has developed long-range weather forecasting techniques that led to some remarkable accomplishments. In World War II, when establishment forecasters said it could not be done, Krick was able to provide military planners with sound weather-wise dates for such crucial operations as the invasion of Normandy, the invasion of North Africa, the strategic bombing of Germany, the crossing of the Rhine.

In this delightful book, author Victor Boesen tells how, since the Eisenhower Administration, Krick has been providing the White House with accurate weather information such as it cannot obtain from Federal forecasters. Boesen documents the careful scientific methods Krick follows in both his long-range forecasting and cloud-seeding operations. Krick's organization doesn't hit the bull's-eye every time, but it has about 85 percent effective results, according to neutral observers.

STORM:
Irving Krick
vs.
the U.S. Weather
Bureaucracy

Victor Boesen

G. P. Putnam's Sons / New York

Library of Congress Cataloging in Publication Data
Boesen, Victor.
Storm: the U.S. weather bureaucracy vs. Irving Krick.
Includes index.
SUMMARY: A biography of the meteorologist who has
helped develop a method to produce accurate long-range
weather forecasts.
1. Krick, Irving. 2. Meteorologists—United States—
Biography. 3. Long-range weather forecasting.
4. Rain-making. [1. Krick, Irving. 2. Meteorologists.
3. Weather forecasting] I. Title.
QC858.K74B6   551.6′092′4   [B]   [92]   77-26726
ISBN 0-399-20636-1

Contents

STORM:
Irving Krick
vs.
the U.S. Weather
Bureaucracy

1

We Need To Know
the Weather

Soon after Jimmy Carter took office as President of the United States, there was a telephone call from Washington, D. C., to the Krick weather service in Palm Springs, California. The call came from Gretchen Poston, social secretary at the White House.

"I wonder if you would be kind enough to do for me what you did for Bess Abell," Mrs. Poston said to Krick. "We plan a number of outside social events—picnics, ballets, luncheons, state dinners, and so forth—and we need to know what the weather is going to be. We'd like to know a month or more ahead."

Krick assured Mrs. Poston, whose friend, Bess Abell, had been social secretary to Mrs. Lyndon Johnson, that he would be honored to serve once again as long-range weather forecaster for the First Family.

The Johnsons had been pleased with his work. "Whether your weather prediction was six days, six weeks, or six months ahead of time, it was always accurate," Bess Abell gratefully wrote Krick at the finish of the Johnson years in the White House. "I leaned on your prediction in selecting the date for the first White House State Dinner in the Rose Garden," she recalled. "I remember it so well—Mr. Choy [Eddie Choy, one of Krick's men] said it would be the perfect night, but the day would give us ulcers—there would be dark clouds and high winds, but no rain.

"How right he was! About four o'clock in the afternoon everyone wanted to move tables, place cards and bouquets inside—but I stood firm by your prediction. At eight o'clock when the guests arrived, it was the lovely, calm and balmy evening you promised. What a beautiful, memorable night it was . . ."

Referring to another of Krick's forecasts, Mrs. Abell continued, "Who else in the world would be able to pick the one day in November for Mrs. Johnson to picnic and hike through the Redwoods under clear skys? For weeks before and after that day it rained, but her day there was perfectly delightful. . . ."

Mrs. Johnson added her own note of thanks to Krick, writing that his "well-known-in-advance predictions have been of invaluable help in planning everything from parties on the White House lawn to picnics on the coast of Maine."

Actually, Krick says, he could have told President Carter five years ago that he would have the kind of day he did for his inauguration—that it would be cold but sunny, allowing him and his family to stroll down Pennsylvania Avenue in comfort after the ceremony. "We couldn't predict who the President would be," Krick said, "but we knew what kind of day it would be."

Krick is an old hand at forecasting the weather for the White House. He began when he predicted the conditions for the inauguration of Dwight D. Eisenhower, following this in turn with the same service for John F. Kennedy and Lyndon Johnson. Krick's abilities had been well-known to Ike, for it was Krick, along with a former student of his at the California Institute of Technology, who forecast the critical five days Eisenhower needed to complete the invasion of Normandy in World War II—holding out for his own forecast even though all the other weathermen involved in this awesome decision, including four Britishers, stood against him, insisting that a five-day forecast was impossible.

Krick, in 1969, also forecast the drought of the 1970s, which for several years dried up the country. And as the dry areas have gotten wider and wider and lasted longer and longer—as Krick had said would happen—the calls for his cloud-seeding services to bring rain have increased from farmers, ranchers, hydroelectric firms, water users everywhere, both at home and overseas.

The clients keep coming to Krick, despite unremitting efforts of the United States Weather Bureau to discredit him. The government claims his methods are "unscientific" and deny that he is able to do the things for which his customers have been paying him handsome fees, some for as long as thirty years.

No man can predict the weather for more than about two days, the Weather Bureau argues. After that, the accuracy of the forecast falls off rapidly.

Krick agrees that the weather can't be forecast beyond two days —by the Weather Bureau. "They have no effective forecast methods," he explains. "They go at it wrong. They deal with effect instead of cause. They haven't recognized that the atmosphere operates as a unit and is controlled by extraterrestrial forces, not by what they observe near the surface. That's only a reflection of all that is going on from the top of the atmosphere down."

Nor have all the satellites fired into space to send back pictures of what's going on in the atmosphere, along with other information, made any difference in the Weather Bureau's forecasting accuracy, Krick maintains, saying disdainfully, "These only mean more misinformation sent out more often to more people."

As for seeding the clouds with silver iodide to increase rain and snow, the government considers this to be of doubtful merit, too. After thirty years or so of trying it, and as two-thirds of the nation's 3,000 counties received emergency relief in what the New York *Times* headlined as the *Worst Drought in Centuries*, it still classified cloud-seeding for more rain as "experimental," needing yet more "research."

The refusal of the government to acknowledge that the question was settled long ago: that cloud seeding is a sound, well-established scientific procedure, Krick contends "has cost this country billions —not millions—*billions*. The catastrophic droughts we've been hit with in the Seventies could have been prevented."

2

Schumann's Concerts in A-Minor

Through no fault of his own, Irving Krick found himself in Hollywood in 1930, the first year of the Great Depression, the heavy-duty hard times that followed the stock market crash of the previous autumn. By this chance circumstance, it is fair to speculate, the world gained a scientist and lost a piano player.

Being in southern California, 400 miles from San Francisco, his birthplace and hometown, he felt less of the undertow of his mother's influence. She was set on a musical career for her only son, whose own learnings, on the other hand, were toward science. This deviated rather sharply from traditional family callings. His father and uncle were bankers, whose forebears came to California from Boston, crossing the plains by Conestoga wagon. His maternal grandfather, Henry Clinton Parkhurst, was a novelist and an editor of the San Francisco *Chronicle*.

There was music in the family. Irving's father played the violin and his mother was a talented pianist. Thus, with both parents musical, his mother had visions of Irving becoming a great artist of the keyboard.

Born on December 20, 1906, eight months after the earthquake and fire that ravaged San Francisco, destroying all of the Krick family's possessions, Irving was not many years out of the cradle when his mother began providing him with piano lessons. She had him study under her own teacher, and with such well-known artists of the day as Fred Maurer and E. Robert Schmidt. By the time he was thirteen, he was giving Sunday afternoon concerts at the University of California's Greek Theater in Berkeley. The Steinway grand piano which his mother bought him at the time is still a cherished possession, gracing the marbled living room of his Moorish mansion in Palm Springs.

Krick's piano playing led to another skill. His facile fingers, made so by hours and hours of racing them up and down the keyboard in arpeggio practice, caught the alert eye of his high school typing teacher. She took him under her wing, and presently he won the state speed typing championship.

When Irving's father died unexpectedly, at the young age of thirty-seven, leaving no insurance, his mother taught music to keep Irving's piano lessons going and to put him and his sister Jeanne, who was five years younger than he, through college.

But, for all the preoccupation with music, something happened to Irving while he was in high school. The phenomenon of radio had appeared, and, in common with many another youngster, he built his own radio station, with the call letters 6CKS. He had been bitten by the bacillus scientificus, never to recover.

Entering the University of California at Berkeley, he selected courses that pointed him toward electrical engineering. In his junior year, however, at the urging of his mother, he switched his major to music. He tried out for the school's Glee Club and toured the Orient with the club as its accompanist and piano soloist. A later tour of the United States by the Glee Club included Carnegie Hall and an appearance at the White House for President Coolidge. In addition, off campus, he gave concerts and accompanied singers, both on the stage and on the air, playing with the NBC Symphony Orchestra.

With his thick shock of jet-black hair sagging over his left eye,

Krick could not have looked more the part of the maestro if he had been picked by Hollywood's Central Casting.

All the same, he decided he wasn't good enough to make it to the top in music and went back to science and engineering. By cramming, he completed two years of physics in one, and graduated from the University of California as a physicist in 1928.

His first contact with meteorology came during his college years. His unit of the ROTC was the Coast Artillery, in those days still considered vital to national defense, and at one summer camp the practice range for moving targets was the Strait of Juan de Fuca, off Fort Worden in Washington.

Firing computations for range and azimuth were based on a standard atmosphere chart for density, and on balloon runs for winds. More often than not, the first shots splashed down short of the target, sailed over it, or plowed the water to one side. Then came the day when the fledgling coast defenders dropped a twelve-inch mortar shell down the funnel of the boat towing the target, badly straining relations with the crew.

Since he was the range officer and responsible for what happened, the incident stuck in Krick's mind. Clearly, they needed to know more about the atmosphere, particularly the winds at the top of mortar or anti-aircraft trajectory. Some years later, as a reserve officer in the coast artillery, he helped to pioneer the use of sounding balloons that sent back upper air information in real time, and worked up better ballistics tables for fire control, in particular high altitude anti-aircraft guns.

After graduating from UC as a physicist, Krick again yielded to his mother's wishes and returned to music. He became assistant manager of Radio Station KTAB in San Francisco, where he had often played the piano, doing programming, disc jockeying, and almost anything else there was to be done. This work lasted until the arrival of a new manager, who told Krick he was worthy of better things and fired him. "One day you'll thank me," he said, with more prescience than he probably realized.

Krick's Uncle Ed at the American Trust Company thought it was time Krick got out of music and found him a job as a runner for Chapman de Wolfe & Company, stockbrokers. Whether this new position was up or down on the scale of worthy work, as it might be seen by the radio station manager, was rendered academic almost before Krick started, by the stock market crash. Runners for stockbrokers became highly dispensable.

Next, Krick sold pianos on a commission basis, now and then playing the instrument in concert. He finally came to the point where he grimly said to himself, "This is my last." His swan song as a public performer would remain in his mind as a sort of milestone through the years—the first movement of Schumann's Concerto in A-Minor, played with the NBC Orchestra.

His mother had not given up, however, and at her insistence Krick went to Denver to attend a so-called master class in piano, conducted by E. Robert Schmidt, who later that year hired him as his assistant for classes in Hollywood—which was how Krick happened to be in Hollywood in 1930.

Being in southern California coupled with his distaste for the work he had been doing with Schmidt, brought Krick to a hard and final decision: He resolved to make science his lifework.

Krick's brother-in-law, Horace Byers, was studying meteorology at the Massachusetts Institute of Technology under the celebrated Swedish meteorologist, Carl G. Rossby (who one day would figure in Krick's life in ways unsuspected). "Look into this field," Byers wrote Krick from MIT. "It's going to be very important to aviation. I can get you a fellowship from Rossby to study here."

Because he had now been out of school a couple of years, Krick enrolled at the California Institute of Technology to refresh himself on math and physics and learn what he could of meteorology before he went east to MIT, at the time the only school in the United States teaching graduate meteorology.

At CalTech, Krick met Dr. Beno Gutenberg, director of the school's seismological laboratory, who was also teaching a course in the structure of the atmosphere. Gutenberg had been a weatherman with the German Army in World War I and took a special interest in young Krick. He gave him a desk in his office and, to supplement his work in the classroom, sent him to study the weather maps at the United States Weather Bureau in Los Angeles.

Gradually Krick began to learn about the atmosphere and how it operated as a worldwide system. Under Gutenberg's influence, he came to think globally in considering what went on atmospherically. He studied the planetary wind systems instead of mere local air movements. He saw that what happened in one place produced an effect elsewhere—that Newton's law of motion was in operation. He realized that trying to solve the mysteries of the weather by studying a small area of the atmosphere is like trying to figure out how a machine works by looking at a single part.

With the big picture in mind, pupil and teacher took up the ideas of Professor Wilhelm Bjerknes of the Geophysical Institute of Bergen, Norway, and his son Jacob. The elder Bjerknes had lectured earlier at CalTech on hydrodynamics. The two Norwegians held that by analyzing air masses of different origins and characteristics—of different temperatures and moisture densities, for example —where the two masses met could be determined and the weather along the boundary predicted.

There was nothing really new about the theory of moving air masses and the practice of drawing a line between them to show where they meet. They had been discovered and written about nearly a century earlier, in 1841, by Professor James Pollard Espy, who drew lines on the weather charts he prepared for the Navy, indicating weather fronts moving across the country, west to east.

But the practice of drawing fronts on weather maps was gradually abandoned. The idea grew that more or less all one needed to foretell the weather was to follow surface barometric pressure patterns on the map. If the patterns were moving in a given direction at, say, 600 miles a day, then it followed that a change of weather would be coming up the next day 600 miles farther down the line. The trouble was, of course, that too often pressure patterns have a habit of slowing down or speeding up, changing direction, and decreasing or increasing their intensity, thus wrecking the forecast.

Yet, this is still essentially the way weather is forecast by government agencies, even now, toward the end of the twentieth century.

Krick showed such promise in science after a year or so at CalTech that Gutenberg persuaded him to give up his plans to attend MIT. "Stay here at CalTech," Gutenberg urged. "I think you have the capability to work with me, and perhaps eventually they'll set up a course in meteorology, either under me or somebody else, and you can become a part of it."

Krick wasn't anxious to leave his native California for Boston anyway, so he stayed. In another year he felt he had learned enough about the weather to put his knowledge to use. With a roll of weather maps under his arm, he presented himself to Jimmie James, chief pilot and vice president of operations for Western Air Express, forerunner of Western Airlines.

James was interested in any system of weather forecasting that promised to improve the chances of flights getting through, and he listened patiently, if skeptically, as his rather dandified young caller expounded on the merits of the Norwegian Air Mass Analysis method of weather forecasting. It was probably just as well that James didn't know he was listening to a piano player.

"Weather is made by the battle always going on between warm air moving up from the tropics and the cold air coming down from the arctic," Krick explained, unrolling his maps on the counter. "Where the two air masses meet, the cold air plows in under the warm air, throwing it upward to where it's cooler and causing it to lose its moisture in the form of rain or snow. We call this boundary between cold and warm air a weather front.

"I see," James nodded, more or less absently.

"If you know where one of these fronts is going to occur," Krick went on, "you can tell a great deal about what the weather is going to be along its length as it moves."

"Your timing is pretty good," James interrupted finally. "Joe

George, our regular meteorologist, is going on vacation. If you want to take a job as a clerk, handling the mail and doing some of the paper work, you can draw those funny-looking maps and help us on the weather in your spare time."

Krick soon became known around Western's terminal in Burbank as "the baggage-slinger." With a pistol strapped to his hip, he toted luggage for the passengers, loaded and unloaded mailbags, and made out the forms that showed the weight of the cargo, an important job in the aviation of 1932, when a few pounds too much could mean disaster.

When there was nothing else to do, he happily talked with the pilots about air masses, giving them insights into how it helped to know about them because of the rough weather frequently found in their vicinity. They were soon listening to his advice. "If you fly at 10,000 feet on the way out and at a different altitude coming back, you'll have a tail wind both ways," Krick would tell them.

It didn't take the airline long to adopt the slogan: "Western Air Express planes always have tail winds."

One day, as pilot Fred Kelly prepared to take off for Salt Lake City, Krick advised him, "There's a cold front just west of Milford, Utah. If you'll sit down at Milford for a couple of hours, the storm will pass to the east and you can go on."

Kelly gratefully reported on his return that he might have been in serious trouble over the Wasatch Mountains but for Krick's warning about the storm. It had been quite turbulent, but spent itself in about the time Krick estimated, allowing Kelly to resume his flight to Salt Lake City.

Krick thereupon was made full-time weatherman for the line, with a free hand to go about forecasting in his own way, unfettered by conventional procedures. He drew lines on the maps showing where air masses came together, causing weather fronts, wind changes, and other effects important for the airman to know about. This innovation upset Joe George when he came back from vacation.

"What are these lines you've been putting on the maps?" George demanded. Krick's explanation failed to mollify him. "Don't mess with the weather maps!" he ordered.

Jimmie James talked the matter over with the pilots, who agreed the lines helped and were a step forward. "I want the lines left in," James ruled.

In the early morning hours of April 4, 1933, Krick's habit of searching out fronts on weather maps involved him in an event which firmly set the course of his future. With an early morning class at CalTech, Krick took a nap each night during the five hours of little flying activity when the 110-miles-an-hour Fokker F-10s flew from Salt Lake City to Las Vegas.

As he turned in, he remarked to the radio operator, "I'm glad we're not flying off the coast of New Jersey tonight. There's a cold front coming down from the northeast and a warm front coming up from the southwest. When the two meet there is going to be one awful mix-up. It'll be very violent."

Krick was no sooner asleep than he was shaken awake by the radioman. "My God, the Akron just went down in the Atlantic off Barnegat Light—right where you said all that rough weather was coming!" he exclaimed.

The Akron was an enormous airship—785 feet long, large enough to accommodate five airplanes aboard. It was the pride of the United States Navy. Seventy-three men died in the disaster, the headline event of the day.

At school later in the morning Krick sought out Dr. Theodore von Karman. Known as "master of the wind" for his knowledge of fluid mechanics, this Hungarian-born scientist was chairman of CalTech's Guggenheim Aeronautics Laboratory, which later was to spawn the world-famous Jet Propulsion Laboratory. Von Karman also headed the Goodyear Airship Institute at Akron, Ohio.

"The Akron never had a chance," Krick said. "The wind shear set up by these two opposing air masses blowing in opposite directions was bound to destroy the ship. She should never have been flown into this kind of weather."

22

Von Karman was impressed by Krick's earnestness. "Get me the velocity of these winds and we'll calculate the stresses on the ship," von Karman told him.

The calculations, by Frank Wattendorf, Karman's assistant, proved Krick to be correct: the Akron, broken in two like a stick across the knee of a giant, was doomed from the moment the ship left the hangar, although the United States Weather Bureau had reported that the storm posed no danger to flying that day.

Von Karman called on Dr. Robert Andrews Millikan, chairman of CalTech's executive council, Nobel laureate for isolating the electron and measuring its charge, thereby opening the way for the age of electronics, and holder of the Roosevelt Association Medal for his discovery of the cosmic ray.

"Chief," von Karman began, addressing Millikan by the title everyone used, "I think commercial aviation is here to stay and that meteorology is going to play a more and more important role in it as time passes. I think we ought to set up some sort of meteorology course for graduate students, maybe with Krick teaching it."

Millikan, who had been General John J. Pershing's weatherman in World War I, agreed. "It's time weather forecasting was improved," he mused. "We need to be able to forecast farther ahead and to be more accurate."

By the fall of 1933, a few months after the Akron disaster, CalTech had a meteorology department, headed by Krick, who had earned his master's degree in Meteorology during the summer. Krick, cultivating a mustache to make him look older than his students, taught courses in the practical side of forecasting while von Karman and Gutenberg dealt in the theoretical aspects of the subject. One of Krick's pupils, incidentally, was Western Air Express' Joe George, sent over by Jimmie James.

Those who filled the classes included students from all branches of the armed services, the United States Weather Bureau, the airlines, and from foreign governments. A frequent visitor was Lieutenant Colonel Henry H. Arnold, commanding officer at March

Air Force Base, at Riverside, California, whose bombers carried Dr. Millikan's cosmic ray equipment on special trips aloft.

In his book, *Global Mission*, published after World War II, Arnold recalled the first time he met Krick, in December 1940, describing it as one of his "most unforgettable contacts with an academic scientist." Krick's analysis of what happened to the doomed Akron and why, had affected him as few other things he "had heard in my twenty years of flying," Arnold wrote. "Naturally, I watched Dr. Krick's work eagerly after that. Weather is the essence of flying."

As a teacher as well as a student, now preparing for his doctorate, Krick was paid $117 a month—not bad pay at a time when some 20 million Americans had no income at all. The money enabled Krick to quit his job at Western Air Express and devote full time to the academic life.

After Krick left the airline, Clancy Dayhoff, its public relations chief, proudly published the claim that during the months Krick forecast the weather for them he had been right 96.4 percent of the time. The best the Weather Bureau had been able to do, Dayhoff wrote, was around 65 percent.

The Weather Bureau was not pleased.

When Krick had received his Ph.D in Meteorology in 1934, Dr. Millikan sent him to Europe. "I want you to visit every meteorology institute you can this summer," Millikan instructed his protégé. "See what they are doing, and when you come back to CalTech this fall I want you perhaps to point our research in a different direction from what everybody else is doing."

In Germany, Krick ran across a meteorologist named Stuve who had some new ideas in getting at the weather's behavior. Figuratively, Stuve worked from the top down, looking down through the atmosphere from above rather than up through it from below, as others were doing. He believed that the heat balance at the outer limits of the atmosphere governed the planetary winds, and that what went on with the weather in the lower portion of the atmosphere was the result of what happened above it.

Stuve's thinking appealed to Krick. It reminded him of Gutenberg's cosmic view of things back at CalTech. It went beyond that of the Norwegians, who were working with contrasting air masses which produced weather as they moved about in the lower atmosphere and collided with one another. Krick asked himself, What moved these masses around in the first place?

What excited Krick most on his tour of Europe's weather laboratories in the summer of 1934 was something he picked up in Leipzig from Professor Gerhard Wieckman, a dissenter from the Nazi movement. Wieckman led Krick into the woods where they could talk freely and told him he had discovered that there was a systematic progression of local barometric pressures which registered on a barograph, an instrument for recording air pressures at the earth's surface.

"I can make long-range forecasts from this," Wieckman said.

Krick returned home convinced that the Germans were closer to long-range weather prediction than anyone else. What he learned that day in the German woods, combined with further researches at CalTech, would have a bearing on the outcome of the coming war.

"I feel there is a good possibility that we will be able to make forecasts that go far out—well beyond where people are working today," Krick told Dr. Millikan, who directed Krick to press on with his studies.

Did the weather behave chaotically, as many argued (and still do), or were there orderly, recurring patterns to it? Krick and his students began to examine the entire complex of wind systems for as much of the globe as they could. By diligent search and persistence they were able to collect weather data going back five years for most of the Northern Hemisphere—Eastern Asia, the Pacific, North America, the Atlantic and Europe.

By the late thirties they had established that they could group barometric pressure patterns and related daily weather in blocks of six days. They found there was a finite number of these patterns, or weather types, as they called them, for each octant of the globe, or for each quadrant of a hemisphere. They were able to classify and catalogue all weather types occurring within the five years they had studied.

The six-day weather types became the building blocks, providing a basis for long-range forecasting. Once a weather type was identified, the weather across one quadrant of the hemisphere could be predicted at any location for the next six days. The pressure configurations for a given type were found to be the same in winter as in summer, irrespective of conditions at the earth's surface. This indicated that control did, indeed, come from the upper atmosphere, far above the earth. However, the weather associated with each pattern changed with the seasons.

Thus, if one could determine the sequence in which these weather types occurred for a month, a season, or years ahead, the way was open to make ultra long-range weather forecasts. Krick and his associates would reach this achievement in the late 1950s.

As they learned more and more in the laboratory, Millikan encouraged Krick to start putting the knowledge to practical use, applying it in the field. "Make what you're doing relevant to society," Millikan counseled. "Without that, it all means nothing."

By chance, this field testing began with the motion picture industry. Homer Seale, manager of the Alhambra Airport, where Western Air Express had first operated, remembered Krick's forecasting score for the airline after a movie crew kept showing up to shoot scenes at the airfield, only to be thwarted by fog each time at great expense to the producers of the film.

With a good ear for the knock of opportunity, Seale called on Krick at CalTech, and soon Krick was weatherman to Hollywood, with Homer Seale working for him. Any reservations the film men may still have had about Krick's gifts as a weather prophet vanished after he picked the night for burning Atlanta in *Gone With The Wind*. It had to be a night that was clear, calm, and without wind, out of consideration for adjacent property. Obviously, there could be no retakes.

26

Word of Krick's work for the film makers soon spread to other industries. A studio worker had a friend with an orange grove, sensitive to frost, and presently Krick was forecasting the weather for the California citrus industry. After he forecast the cold January of 1937, which wiped out much of the crop, citrus growers called him from Arizona, Texas and Florida, as well.

The Detroit Edison Company was troubled by ice storms which downed its power lines. Was there anything Krick could do about that from California? Krick not only told them when the next ice storm would hit, but warned that it would be highly unusual, bringing lightning along with the ice to knock out transformers.

This feat brought more utilities to his door, followed by oil companies, farmers, ranchers, aerial surveyors, construction firms, dam builders, department stores, sports promoters. Yachtsmen sailing to Hawaii during the annual race to the islands asked about the weather en route. Radio stations began broadcasting his predictions. In time, after World War II, the Red Cross wanted to know about hurricanes, floods, tornadoes, and other such calamities a year in advance, so they could be on hand with help for the victims when the trouble came.

Even undertakers had use for Krick: they needed to know how deep the ground would be frozen, for the benefit of their gravediggers.

As the demand for Krick's services increased, Weather Bureau men began dogging his footsteps, prodded by Dr. Carl Rossby, the former head of MIT's meteorology department. Rossby had come to grief after he received an ultimatum from the chief of the Air Force Weather Service, Captain Robert M. Losey, a former student of Krick's, that unless Rossby adopted Krick's training methods for his own Air Force students he would get no more of them.

Rossby, who regarded Krick as an upstart, refused—and was fired. His pride was further ruffled when his place was given to Dr. Sverre Petterssen of Norway, who had lectured at CalTech at the invitation of Krick, Petterssen's pupil for six weeks during Krick's

1934 visit to Europe. Finding a new job as Assistant Chief of the United States Weather Bureau for Education, Rossby warned against Krick and set up a half-dozen competing weather schools at colleges and universities, including one at the University of California at Los Angeles, twenty miles from CalTech.

Weather Bureau men told Krick's clients and potential clients that his methods were not "scientific." At best, they said, Krick's theories were "experimental," as yet without basis in sound scientific truth. "Beware of the salesman scientist," they cautioned.

The Weather Bureau tried to lure his customers away by offering a specialized service of its own each time Krick added a new category of service. In so doing, The Los Angeles *Times* noted, the Weather Bureau became "the first government forecasting bureau in the nation to offer a teletype system whereby information of interest to a particular group is 'piped' directly into the offices of the latter."

Many of the defectors to the government's bait were soon back in Krick's fold, happy again to pay handsome fees for what the Weather Bureau offered free but failed to deliver. "It's obvious we wouldn't pay for his forecasts year after year if we could get equally accurate and detailed predictions free from the bureau," one client remarked.

Frustrated and jealous, Weather Bureau officials slashed at Krick in print. "Now, of course, there is nothing whatever to distinguish Dr. Krick from scads of other self-seekers who choose to prostitute their talents in the assiduous effort to satisfy the maddening crowd's well-known appetite for exploitation and ballyhoo," wrote Tom Reed, Weather Bureau chief in San Francisco, in the publication *United States Air Services*, July, 1935. At the time Krick was twenty-eight and had just been hired by American Airlines to upgrade the line's weather service.

"What does distinguish him from the rest of the horn-blowing chorus," Reed went on, "is the exalted academic altitude from which he does the blowing. When he wallows in the muck of cheap and noisy self-exploitation, he splashes with his own advertising ooze a high-class and eminently respectable lycée."

The Weather Bureau's gratuitous solicitude for what Krick might be doing to CalTech's reputation was not shared by Dr. Millikan. "I feel quite sure that there is no one who has done more toward improving meteorology than has Irving Krick," Millikan wrote to Dr. F. B. Jewett, head of the Bell Laboratories at American Telephone and Telegraph, who had helped CalTech get free teletype service from the Weather Bureau, but who now had complaint from a critic that other schools, such as MIT, paid for theirs.

Millikan assured Jewett that CalTech wanted no special favors. "Let us know what the regular pay basis is and I will do what I can to meet the conditions," he wrote.

In a postscript, Millikan added edgily, "The fact which Mr. Powley [the critic] mentions, that the movie and citrus industries have desired to pay Krick something for giving them forecasts sufficiently superior to those that they can get through the Weather Bureau for nothing to make them want to pay for his in preference, has, of course, nothing whatever to do with the problem; though I suspect that jealousy of Krick's success on the part of some Weather Bureau officials has had something to do with Mr. Powley's letter."

Likewise coming to Krick's defense was science writer William S. Barton of The Los Angeles *Times*. "Dr. Krick, unless he'd hid abroad à la Lindbergh, no more could have escaped getting his name in print than any American who does something first, be it flying the Atlantic, starting a frog farm or, in this case, founding an interesting new industry of selling weather."

"Let's see how Dr. Krick's predictions have been turning out," Barton continued. "In yesterday's article in the *Times* it was pointed out that the Los Angeles office of the Weather Bureau was considered by the reporter to have been wrong seven times straight in its afternoon forecasts . . . On five of those days rain fell that the bureau failed to predict." Krick, on the other hand, had predicted rain for each of those five days, Barton wrote.

On another day, Barton went on, "when a near-flood of two inches of rain fell, Krick predicted, 'cloudy and heavy rain,' while the Bureau predicted, 'partly cloudy with light showers.'"

As for the propriety of the Weather Bureau supplying the kind of specialized service Krick provided, Barton asked, "What of the taxpayer? Should the Weather Bureau be expanded to the point where it is spending half its time telling motion picture companies what make up tints its extras will require two weeks from now? . . .

"The most important question remains to be answered, Will a more sympathetic attitude on the part of the public and a more progressive outlook by government weather men serve the good and the safety of the nation?" Barton concluded.

In marked contrast to the stance of the Weather Bureau toward Krick were the things his clients were saying. "Now that we have (your system)," wrote President C. R. Smith of American Airlines, "I wonder how we ever got along without it."

"Your forecasts have been hitting us right between the eyes," wrote Marshall Field & Company in Chicago. General Manager Arnold Eddy of the University of Southern California sent word of "how perfectly your predictions came true during the current football season . . . We grade you an 'A'."

"We are now on our second year of using your long-range forecasting service and I wish . . . to compliment you on the accuracy of your forecasts," said the New York-Alaska Gold Dredging Corporation of Seattle. From the Delco Appliance Division of the General Motors Corporation, Rochester, New York: ". . . Your ability to forecast well in advance of actual conditions with as high a degree of accuracy as you achieved last year is very surprising."

Commonwealth & Southern Corporation of Birmingham, Alabama, generating more than 100 million kilowatt-hours a week, mostly with water power, had found Krick's monthly rain forecasts for the Coosaw River "at least 75 percent accurate." Fruit and vegetable growers, the James G. McCarrick Company of Robstown, Texas, wanted "to thank you for the service rendered us from your long-range forecasts the past two years." The forecasts had helped both in harvesting and planting and "also in determining our movement of vegetables through the stormy periods."

The Anderson-Tully Company, of Memphis, writing of how helpful Krick's forecasts had been to their business of logging, hoped that his efforts to improve the weather service "will be encouraged by the Federal Government. If war should come, as it well might, long-range weather forecasting would be of the utmost importance . . . to our national defense."

There was no way to top the words of William C. Ackerman, graduate manager of the "Associated Students" of the University of California in Los Angeles. "In all of the forecasts made for us during . . . [the two years they had been using Krick's forecasts] Dr. Krick has been 100 percent correct in his predictions," Ackerman wrote, commenting, "The University would be very much interested in any help that might be given Dr. Krick to accelerate his long-range forecasting research at the California Institute of Technology."

Oliver L. Parks, president of Parks Air College, an aviation school in St. Louis, Missouri, sent word, "We have talked at considerable length with certain Air Corps officers about the success of the forecasts. I hope you get proper appropriations to carry on your fine work."

The California Division of Highways, concerned with snows in the mountains, had this to say: "The experience we have had with the long-range prediction proves ever more convincing that such service is necessary in order that storm damage to our state highway system can be kept to a minimum."

Referring to several recent storms, the highway authorities continued, "The accurate timing and indication of their intensity enabled us to prepare for them to a greater extent than would otherwise have been done, the saving from damage to us at that time more offsetting the cost of your service for a long period of time."

To the Appalachian Electric Power Company in Charleston, West Virginia, Krick's service "has practically become indispensable . . . we now wonder how we ever got along without it."

Chief engineer H. E. Hedger of the Los Angeles County Flood Control District, operating sixteen dams, sixteen debris basins, six water spreading grounds, more than 500 miles of channels, and three main river outlets to the ocean, wrote, "We have found your short range forecasts extremely helpful," and that Krick's long-range predictions had "created a considerable saving to the District. . . . Any program which you may be able to develop to further increase the efficiency of weather forecasts has our hearty endorsement."

On the strength of Krick's forecast that it would rain, Larry MacPhail, president of the Brooklyn Dodgers, bought $10,000 worth of insurance as protection against rain of more than one-twentieth of an inch between eleven o'clock and two for a certain baseball game. It did rain, as Krick predicted, and the ball club collected on its insurance. The club, MacPhail wrote, made a net profit for the season on week-ahead forecasts of this type from Krick.

There were, of course, some misses, too, in those beginning days —as there still are. "We're not perfect," Krick readily acknowledges. There was the time Humphrey Bogart entered his boat, the *Santana*, in the annual yacht race to Ensenada, Mexico, and asked Krick's office for a weather forecast.

"I want to know about any special conditions I can take advantage of," Bogart growled.

Krick himself was in Europe at the time, but his staff worked up a forecast that should have helped Bogart get to Mexico in winning time. "When you leave San Pedro," the Krick men instructed, "sail out beyond Catalina Island—get out into the open ocean. You'll have a following wind out there that will take you all the way to Ensenada."

Bogart did as directed, sailing well past Catalina—and ran into a dead calm. For three days the *Santana* sat there like Coleridge's "painted ship upon a painted ocean." Bogart never did get to Ensenada.

And, although Krick would one day distinguish himself for his military forecasts, he got off to a rather inauspicious start in this area, badly flubbing his very first prediction.

It happened soon after he began teaching at CalTech. Colonel Arnold invited him for lunch at March Field, and since it wasn't every day that the base entertained a college professor, least of all a dapper, outgoing youngster like this one, the food was preceded by a number of high-octane martinis.

When the lunch ended, Colonel Arnold mentioned that they were flying a training mission to Santa Barbara and back next day. "What's the weather going to be, Doc?" Colonel Arnold asked.

"Hell, no problem," Krick replied expansively, aware through the martinis that the weather front which had passed through the day before was now over in Arizona on its way east. "You'll have no problem at all—fine flying weather."

Back at school next morning, looking at the weather map for the day, Krick was suddenly aghast to see that the front which had been safely over in Arizona the day before, had pulled a once-in-a-blue-moon surprise and reversed itself, looping back to California. With gusty winds and driving rain, it was no day for even the birds to fly.

"I'll never forget it," Krick says, still able to feel embarrassment over the incident these many years later. "It's a wonder General Arnold ever came back to me for anything, but he never mentioned this affair in all the years we knew each other—never a word about it. He was that kind of man."

3

I Want That for the Military

By the end of 1940, knowing the military implications of what was being learned in CalTech's meteorology division under Krick's direction, Millikan and von Karman invited General Arnold—he was now a general and head of the Air Force—to drop in next time his flying missions around the country brought him to the Pasadena area.

Arriving in December, Arnold walked into Krick's laboratory just as Krick read a telegram from a Christmas tree company in Newfoundland that had wanted to know how much time was left to get a cutting of trees out of the woods before they were buried under a fresh snowfall.

"Your forecast's right on the nose," the grateful client wired, going on to say that they had gotten the last trees out just as the first flakes began falling.

Krick handed the wire to General Arnold. "Gee, how do you do that?" asked Arnold, who knew that because of German submarines prowling the Atlantic, Newfoundland was blacked out to weather reports. "How can you forecast the weather in a place where you're not getting any observations?"

"With our weather types we can get by without many observations," Krick answered. "We can go into an area downwind from our types and develop a fairly good forecast without them."

Arnold thought a moment, then broke into the grin that made him known as "Hap." He said, "I want that for the military. Would you set up a special course in long-range forecasting for some of my guys you've trained? Select any four that you want, and I'll grab them from wherever they are and send them to you."

Krick chose four of his most promising former students from the Army Air Corps and gave them a special course in what had been learned since they graduated, including how to forecast for a blacked out region such as Newfoundland. There would be many of those for the United States if war came.

In October, 1941, at the request of General Arnold, who was anxious to make the Weather Bureau more familiar with Krick's work as it was being developed for the Air Force, Krick went to Washington and gave a series of lectures to the government forecasters. He won no converts to his ideas.

With the country now at war, the Air Force in February, 1942, ordered the lectures published for distribution to its weather officers throughout the world. But the man charged with their distribution, Dr. Harry Wexler, a former Weather Bureau employee commissioned for service in the Air Force, locked the documents away, never to be seen.

Far from getting the Weather Bureau's ear, Krick presently found himself on the receiving end of a lecture himself from the bureau's chief, F. W. Reichelderfer. Krick thus was hoist with his own petard, incidentally, for it was he who had recommended Reichelderfer, a one-time Navy weatherman, for his post, acting through Dr. Millikan, former chairman of President Roosevelt's Advisory Committee on the Weather Bureau.

Reichelderfer had been upset by "recent press notices in which you [Krick] were credited with new discoveries in methods of long-range forecasting making it possible to forecast with a high degree of accuracy for periods up to ten years."

In the wake of these stories, Reichelderfer continued with a note of distress, the bureau had received a flood of questions from newsmen and government departments wanting to know where the Weather Bureau stood on long-range forecasting and its use by the military.

"You know that our purpose is to aid and encourage progress in this extremely important phase of weather forecasting," Reichelderfer wrote on December 5, 1941, two days before Pearl Harbor. "Headlines claiming great accuracy in long-range forecasting arouse controversy and are not conducive to real progress."

Reichelderfer recalled impatiently that he had spoken to Krick about this matter twice before, the first time on a visit to CalTech during the summer, and again no longer ago than September.

"I emphasize that I would not like to see you count too much upon your present methods," he wrote. He stressed that Krick's methods were "still experimental."

Caution was the watchword. "If you are on the verge of an enduring technique we shall be very glad, but if it does not turn out as you expect you will suffer and so will the profession." Reichelderfer advised that "for your own protection you ought to get someone to make a thorough statistical check of your latest method." And the agent to do that, Reichelderfer indicated, was the United States Weather Bureau.

Reichelderfer enclosed a copy of the reply he had prepared for all those who wanted to know about long-range forecasting after reading in the newspapers about Krick's work. In the statement Reichelderfer dismissed long-range forecasting as a military tool.

He conceded that "defense needs have multiplied several-fold the importance of extended weather forecasts," adding in passing that this had been "a subject of intense human interest since time immemorial," and he told what the Weather Bureau was doing to foretell the weather further in advance, but said it hadn't made much headway—just as no one else had, either.

"Long-range weather forecasts for periods greatly in excess of those issued by official meteorological organizations," the statement continued, "are somewhat like anticipations of stock market fluctuations—they should be carefully checked for a few months at least before one puts much money in them."

The long-range forecasting claims by the German military, published in the United States shortly before Hitler invaded Poland and set off World War II, had been carefully studied by our own weathermen, both government and private, and had been found to be nothing to get excited about.

Reichelderfer hoped "that the encouragement and effort now being given to research" in forecasting would lead to improvement. "Naturally," he wrote, closing the subject, "the Weather Bureau will adopt long-range forecast methods as soon as reliable techniques are developed."

Then came Pearl Harbor. Krick received a phone call from General Arnold. "Will you come and help us during the war?"

Krick would soon be in uniform. Meanwhile, he was already doing work considered of great value in the struggle ahead—until he received a stunning telegram from the Weather Bureau in Washington saying that because of the war his teletype service was being cut off. "This telegram will serve as notice of cancellation of your present agreement for connection on Schedule C, effective 12:01 AM Eastern Standard Time, December 24, 1941," the message read. "Necessity for this action regretted."

Krick wired General Arnold in Washington, asking his help in having an exception made in CalTech's case, "so that training program here can continue uninterrupted as well as our liaison with the Air Corps weather research center at Bolling Field for purpose of providing them with essential weather forecasts."

Krick then wired each of his clients apprising them of what had happened and saying, "This jeopardizes our defense training program as well as all weather advices to military services, air carriers, and essential defense industries." He asked that they wire him a statement collect, affirming their need for CalTech's forecasts.

But Krick's efforts to have his teletype connections with the Weather Bureau came to nothing. At midnight, Christmas Eve, 1941, the machines were cut off as scheduled. "Now what are you going to do, Dr. Krick?" taunted a little note at the end of the final transmission.

The day after Christmas, however, Krick received fleeting hope that the service might be restored. President Roosevelt issued an executive order placing the issuance of weather information under the Secretary of Commerce for the duration of the war. Under the President's order the chief of the Weather Bureau would act as liaison officer, linking the Commerce Secretary with the Secretaries of War and Navy.

That sounded to Krick as if the Secretary of Commerce became boss of the Weather Service. But that was not the way Weather Bureau Chief Reichelderfer made it out. "This executive order," he wrote in a circular which he hastily distributed to all weather bureau stations on December 29, "places the Weather Bureau in closer relationship with the War and Navy Departments. . . . It means that the weather services directly related to the war efforts of the Nation are our paramount duty."

What the Weather Bureau saw as its expanded responsibilities apparently included keeping an eye on Irving Krick. Ostensibly at the request of the military, soon after the Weather Bureau had his teletypes disconnected. Reichelderfer took steps to block Krick from giving a paper which he was scheduled to deliver before a meeting of the American Institute of the Aeronautical Sciences in New York at the end of January, 1942.

Reichelderfer gave as his reason that the paper contained information "which might be of value to the enemy," presumably seeing no inconsistency between this and the bureau's position all along that Krick's work had no value. Making sure as well that

Krick's words wouldn't be read, Reichelderfer also asked the Institute of Aeronautical Sciences "not to publish Dr. Krick's manuscript until it has been released by the Weather Bureau with the consent of military authorities."

As to the problem raised by losing his teletype tickers, Krick resourcefully found an answer. He supplied aneroid barometers to his subscribers, asking them to send him the daily pressure readings in their respective areas. This was all he needed.

This remedy for the loss of the teletypes went awry a few times, as when the Detroit Edison Company first checked with the Weather Bureau to see if it was all right to send Krick the information he wanted. The Weather Bureau said no, ignoring Krick's protest that the bureau itself continued to publish weather information in the daily newspapers.

However the Weather Bureau might rate Krick's talents, the Army and Navy were engaged in something of a tug of war for his services. Although he held a reserve Ensign's commission in the Navy, the Army felt it had first call on him: through General Arnold it felt he belonged to the Army by right of discovery. It wanted him both to operate a weather forecasting plan developed with his help for the Air Forces and to carry out an extensive program of further research in long-range forecasting.

Arnold, Army Deputy Chief of Staff for Air, gave the issue his personal attention, taking it up with Admiral Harold R. Stark, Chief of Naval Operations. "Active duty status now appears necessary to make essential information available to him and to use his capacities to the utmost," Arnold wrote. "The position to which his assignment is contemplated requires the rank of Major in the Army or Lieutenant Commander in the Navy. Therefore, it is requested that he be promoted to this comparable rank in the Navy and detailed to the Army for assignment to the Army's Weather Research Center."

If this arrangement didn't suit the Navy, Arnold went on, "it is requested that Dr. Krick's reserve commission in the Navy be terminated in order to make him available to the Army for commissioning and assignment to active duty."

The Navy refused either to give up its man or to promote him. "The Bureau of Aeronautics is desirous of retaining this officer in the Navy," Admiral Stark replied, writing that he himself agreed that the Navy should keep Krick so long as he was made available to the Air Forces. But that was as far as he could go, Stark wrote.

Krick was too young at thirty-three to be promoted to lieutenant commander, the admiral indicated. The best the Navy could do was to make him a senior lieutenant.

Dr. Millikan, who had wanted Krick to keep his civilian status, believing he could serve better that way, took a tactful hand on Krick's side. In a letter to Reichelderfer, Millikan wrote that he thought the arrangements worked out by General Arnold to make use of Krick's talents within the Air Forces were "excellent."

"I think you and I are fully agreed that Krick's techniques are sufficiently promising to warrant further intensive and scientific study and development," Millikan wrote. "I do not know myself of any other monthly forecasts which have actually been made so as to get a comparison. If he has stimulated others to do as well, he is making the biggest contribution that has ever been made to meteorology . . ."

In Washington Krick began his military service as a naval lieutenant heading the Army Air Force's long-range forecasting section, as General Arnold had wanted. With Hitler still having his way in Europe, it was highly important to deliver combat airplanes to the other side of the Atlantic as fast as possible, and one of Lieutenant Krick's first duties was to pick the days, a week in advance, when planes could be safely flown across the ocean. It was, of course, not as simple in 1942 as in the coming jet age when planes could fly farther and faster and above the weather.

In their respective war rooms, Krick also briefed Air and Army intelligence officers once a week on the possible influence of upcoming weather on both Allied and enemy capabilities.

Gradually, the military high command came to see that they couldn't simply plan an activity for a certain day without taking the weather into account. This was all the more true if the activity called for air and ground forces to work together. It would become the procedure, insofar as possible, first to determine what the weather was going to be, then suit the combat missions to it.

4

This Is the Day
the Japs Will Attack

"The Japs have gone on radio silence up in the North Pacific," an Army intelligence officer remarked to Krick one day in late May, 1942. "What do you make of that?"

Krick studied the weather maps for the region and saw that there was a cold front between the place where the enemy had been known to be, and the Aleutian Islands, curving southwestward in a long arc from the Alaskan mainland. He knew that our own planes, flying reconnaissance out of Alaska, were unable to penetrate this cold front without icing up and therefore wouldn't know what the enemy was up to.

"They could be planning to attack the Aleutians," Krick said. He studied the maps further, then he stuck his forefinger on the calendar and said, "This is the day they'll attack Dutch Harbor—June 3."

The intelligence officer reported the conversation to his chief, General George Strong, who rushed Krick before General George C. Marshall, Army Chief of Staff. Marshall immediately ordered an airlift of troops and supplies to Alaska, so that when the Japanese attacked, hitting Dutch Harbor with four bombers and about fifteen fighters on the very day Krick had predicted, the Americans were ready. The raid "was not a surprise and the station was prepared to meet it," reported Rear Admiral C. S. Freeman, commandant of the 13th Naval District, as quoted by the United Press.

Afterward, Army staff intelligence asked and received verification of the accuracy of Krick's Alaska forecast.

Weather Bureau Chief Reichelderfer, knowing nothing about that forecast, meantime kept after him. In a long memorandum to Krick the day after the forecast was verified, Reichelderfer repeated that he considered long-range forecasting humbug, no better than "those to be expected by random process, that is, without skill."

Indeed, Reichelderfer wrote, "None of the long-range methods now under development by the Joint Weather Central [a grouping of Army, Navy, and Weather Bureau forecasters under the Weather Bureau's roof, all making their own forecasts] is as yet appreciably superior to pure guesswork for periods beyond three or four days."

The fact that there had been acceptance of Krick's work, Reichelderfer went on, presumably having in mind Krick's paying clients, wasn't enough to prove anything. "For example [astrologers] enjoy a popular reputation for farsightedness, yet their predictions have been proven valueless."

He repeated an old theme: "All long range forecasting methods are still highly experimental. . . . The emphasis you are placing on long range forecasts for military purposes is potentially dangerous since it may lead military commanders to place undue reliance upon doubtful forecasts. Vital decisions may be at stake."

Vital decisions were indeed at stake, and General Arnold, much impressed by Krick's Alaska forecast, wanted him in Air Force uniform. He wrote to Admiral Ernest J. King, commander in chief of the Navy, asking for Lieutenant Krick's release.

In no time Krick was out of the Navy and in the Air Force, but only with the rank of major, inferior to the colonels—his former students—he would be working with. Moreover, his old antagonist, the Weather Bureau, dominated the military weather services, and those officers not already in line with the Bureau's thinking soon succumbed to it. This included Colonel Don Zimmerman, whom Krick had recommended to Arnold to head the weather directorate.

The situation boded ill for General Arnold's hopes of providing long-range weather information to all branches of the Army in all parts of the world. Typically, when Krick undertook to distribute thirty-day forecasts of the kind for which business, industry, and agriculture had paid him high fees for years, he was blocked from doing so. One after another of his ideas for getting his speciality of long-range forecasting put to use in the country's defense was either turned down outright or allowed to pass without action.

One of the pivotal decisions at stake in the autumn of 1942 was the Allied invasion of North Africa. The man chosen to lead the Africa landings at Casablanca was General George H. Patton, who knew that the sea alone could defeat him if he struck at the wrong time.

"While I'm on the Atlantic going toward Casablanca," Patton bluntly told the Navy's weathermen, "I want to know what the sea and swell height and wave action on the beach are going to be when we get there. And I want to know a month before! Can you tell me?"

The Navy replied that it could not—that nobody could. A forecast that far ahead was impossible.

Patton discussed the problem with General Strong. "There's a man in the Air Force who might be able to do something for you," Strong replied, thinking of Krick. "He's from the California Institute of Technology and has some new ideas that seem to work."

"Send him over to see me," Patton directed.

Before setting out, Krick checked with Colonel Zimmerman, his commanding officer. "General Patton wants me to come over and try to tell him how the sea and swell forecast will be for his invasion of Africa," Krick explained. "The Navy has indicated no expertise in the situation."

"You can't do that," Zimmerman objected. "That's the Navy's

job. Anything having to do with the ocean, that's Navy. We can't interfere."

"I'll tell General Patton," Krick replied as he departed.

General Patton knew a great deal about the sea and its behavior off Africa; it was much like the water off Southern California. "Can you forecast the waves, tides, and that sort of thing?" he asked Krick.

"We can give you a general idea of these conditions a month in advance," Krick answered. "We'll update as we go along, and a few days before you land we'll be able to give you the information right on the mark."

Krick paused. "But I understand the Navy is responsible for providing such information and I have been instructed by my commanding officer not to involve the Air Force," he said.

Patton pondered briefly. "Who's this guy that's your superior?" he demanded.

Hesitating, Krick answered, "Zimmerman."

Patton swept up the telephone and called Colonel Zimmerman. "This is General Patton," he announced. "I have Major Krick here with me. I'm going to set up a special unit to make the sea and swell forecast for Operation Torch—and you, you sonofabitch, if you interfere with him I'll have your head in the basket!"

When Krick returned to his office, Zimmerman angrily ordered him confined to his desk. There began a succession of memoranda from Zimmerman to Krick. "You are hereby informed that any further actions on your part contrary to accepted Army policy will result in a request for your relief from active duty," threatened the first.

There was a second memo the same day. "It is directed that you draw a synoptic map, daily, except Sunday, while in Washington."

"You are directed to reply by indorsement hereon stating why you submitted a weather study to G-2, General Staff . . . in disregard of written and verbal directives indicating that all such studies should go through the Director Weather," Zimmerman commanded in a third memo, next day.

In the Army one speaks to God only through St. Peter, Krick was learning—even though, in this case, God had spoken first.

Krick's endorser, a colonel and therefore Zimmerman's equal, explained that Krick had only been following orders to send his study directly to General J. E. Hull, in charge of planning the Africa landings, skipping routine procedures. The endorsing colonel cautioned Zimmerman that Krick was to go on bypassing channels so that "the project he is working on be not handled in a manner which in any way can compromise the secrecy thereof."

Further to nail down the point with Zimmerman, General Strong, as senior security officer for the War Department, intervened in the matter. He telephoned Zimmerman that Krick was to have complete freedom of action. "You are directed to authorize Major Krick to go on dealing through direct channels," General Strong ordered.

Saying nothing of having heard from General Strong, Colonel Zimmerman next day relieved Krick of his command through the device of realigning his long-range forecast section so that he no longer had authority over it and was left with only two of his CalTech colleagues. Krick was close to being out of business.

Meanwhile, the harassing memoranda to Krick went on. "It is directed that you make no further presentations in the Air War Room," Zimmerman wrote on September 12, 1942. "Your name, this date, is being removed from the last of officers eligible to make presentations."

Krick's presentations dealt with long-range forecasting, ordained by Weather Bureau men to be considered "experimental," to remain so until proved otherwise. Since it had taken the Weather Bureau a number of years to adopt the Norwegian Air Mass Analysis system as standard for short-range forecasting, the outlook for the use of long-range forecasting as a tool of war was further dimmed by having Krick stop talking about it.

The memos from the colonels went on tediously. In slack moments, when there were no memoranda to write to Krick, the colonels wrote memos to one another about him.

There was a fearful flap one morning when Krick couldn't be found for a while. He had been in the barbershop.

As the turmoil over Krick's work for General Patton continued, General Arnold's displeasure with the quality of the forecasting coming out of Joint Weather Central deepened. He called Krick to his office to see what could be done about upgrading it. Krick discreetly brought Colonel Zimmerman along.

"I think the Air Force should do the forecasting for the ground forces," General Arnold declared.

Zimmerman quickly objected, as he had objected to the Air Force forecasting for the African operation. "The Air Force should not become involved in any forecasting outside its own requirements," he argued. "The ground forces should do their own. Their requirements are entirely different."

"How are you going to coordinate air and ground if you have two different forecasts?" Krick demanded as Arnold listened. "You'll have as many forecasts as there are meteorologists. When the Air Force has to support the ground forces, the Air Force should make the forecasts, or the ground should—one or the other, but not both."

"I want the Air Force to do it," General Arnold said quietly.

Zimmerman went on being disputatious.

"Get the hell out of here, Zimmerman!" Arnold suddenly ordered.

As Zimmerman retreated, Arnold said to Krick, "I want you to prepare a plan for operational weather services for all branches of the Army—maybe even the combined forces and ultimately all Allied forces—which the Air Force can run and be responsible for."

"Maybe you would like to wait and see if we flub the forecast for the Africa landings," Krick replied, half jokingly. "You may want to kick me out and let me go back to my work at CalTech."

Krick drew up a plan whereby the weather service for all branches of the armed forces would be coordinated under a single head, with the Air Force in charge. The plan was endorsed by several generals in addition to Arnold, who put it aside to await the opportune time for its implementation.

Meantime, with motives known only to themselves, Krick's superiors at Weather Central sent an urgent telegram to Dr. Millikan at CalTech, asking his opinion on forecasts longer than ten days. "Request immediate answer within twelve hours via Western Union to Colonel Smith, Assistant Director of Weather, Weather Bureau Building, Washington, D. C.," the message directed. It bore the names "Smith" and "Zimmerman."

In two and a half hours Dr. Millikan's reply was on its way by night letter. "There are no scientific reasons for thinking that long-range forecasting may not be developed into a reasonably reliable procedure," Millikan wired. ". . . The theory of weather types, which we regard as already a definitely established fact, makes possible a precise mathematical formulation of the problem of long-range forecasting . . ."

Millikan explained how this formulation was reached and said that while more needed to be known, "there are enough encouraging indications to justify very intensive attack on the problem . . ."

Millikan's message bore the name of Paul S. Epstein in addition to his own. Epstein had been characterized by President Karl Compton of MIT as "the dean of American theoretical physicists."

Millikan wrote two letters to General Arnold, including the message from the Colonels. In praise of Krick he wrote:

"A number of us who had a chance to observe the work of Dr. Krick for the past ten years . . . have been impressed by the sanity and intelligence of his approach to meteorological problems as we saw them . . . We had also become pretty thoroughly convinced that he was introducing some new methods which had a good deal of promise for the ultimate development of very valuable long-range forecasts . . ."

In his second letter to Arnold, Millikan included this striking comment by Epstein:

"Before Krick's theory of weather types and sequences was advanced, the problem of long-range forecasting was so vague and diffuse as to be altogether hopeless. But with the help of Krick's theory (which I, personally, regard not as a theory but as an established fact) the problem *can be given a precise mathematical formulation.*"

5

The Sea Will Be Failing

For the landings along the coast of French Morocco in North Africa, General Patton called for at least three days with sea swells below eight feet. The weather where the boats were putting in should be clear so that the Air Force could support the landings, dropping men and supplies. Once the landings were committed, there could be no turning back.

At the same time, to the east and north, where enemy aircraft would strike from, it would be well to have cloudiness that screened the landings from air attack until they were well under way and Allied airfields were established. It was a demanding order.

Krick talked things over with Professor H. H. Sverdrup, Director of the Scripps Institution of Oceanography at La Jolla, California, an expert on Pacific Sea swell prediction. Combining Professor Sverdrup's expertise in sea behavior with his own in long-range weather prediction, Krick, on October 17, prepared a chart for transmission to General Patton aboard the flagship of Operation Torch. It showed that the combination of conditions desired would occur between November 7 and November 14. On the seventh, the sea would be at a peak of fifteen feet, extremely high for that time of year, but it would be falling, reaching five feet or less by the fourteenth of the month.

As it turned out, the peak came on November 5, two days early. If the time of the peak had been two days late instead, the landings could have been a disaster. But they were successfully carried out beginning on November 8.

Following the success of the sea and swell forecasts for Operation Torch, a number of Air Force weathermen were trained in the method used. They were assigned to perform this function for all amphibious landings for the rest of the war. Two such specialists were stationed in the British Admiralty to handle the task for the Allies during the invasion of Normandy.

So far as Colonel Zimmerman was concerned, however, Krick was a total loss. As General Patton's tanks pushed farther into Africa and started the enemy on his long retreat, Zimmerman characterized his performance as "unsatisfactory" in the four efficiency report categories of handling officers and men, performance of field duties, administrative and executive duties and leadership.

In the space provided for "a brief general estimate of this officer in your own words," Zimmerman wrote, among other things, that Krick "has repeatedly disregarded instructions to deal through established military channels. In my judgment he is also disloyal and unreliable. In comparing this officer with all other officers of his grade and component known to me, I would place him among the lower third." Had these deficiencies been brought to Krick's attention before this report was written? "Yes," Zimmerman wrote. Had there been any improvement? "None."

General Arnold dissented with Zimmerman. Glancing at the report, he quickly drew a heavy line through the middle of the sheet and boldly wrote, "EXCELLENT—SUPERIOR!" and signed his name.

With the invasion of Africa smoothly launched, General Arnold severed all connections with the Weather Bureau and removed the

Air Force men who had been housed under its roof. He relieved Colonel Zimmerman as chief of the Air Force Weather Bureau Directorate and, on Krick's recommendations, named Colonel Hunt Bassett, another former Krick student, to take his place. Colonel Bassett formed a "Weather Information Section," commanded by yet another former student of Krick's—Colonel Don Yates.

"Okay," Arnold told Krick after these changes had been made, "what do you need now to implement your plan?"

"I want forty years of Northern Hemisphere daily weather maps which we can study and classify before I tackle anything beyond what we're doing now," Krick replied. He felt that the Axis powers had such maps going back at least that number of years. "I'll need about forty men. I'll go back to CalTech and with Millikan's co-operation set up a map analysis unit. The Air Force students who are there can help. We'll have wirephoto and teletype communication with the Signal Corps in Washington and make forecasts for all theaters of war while we're doing the maps. Hell, it will be just as though we were sitting in Washington, but without the static. We can get some work done."

In two weeks, becoming known as "Long-Range Forecast Unit A," Krick and his people were busy at CalTech. They occupied the entire Astrophysics building along with Culbertson Hall, the school auditorium—all gladly turned over to them by Dr. Millikan.

General Arnold arranged with the Weather Bureau to plot daily data on hemispheric base maps from 1899 to 1940. The maps were then analyzed with fronts and isobars (lines connecting all points with the same barometric pressure) by Krick and his crew and by the meteorology group at New York University, each group taking twenty years of maps.

The maps were drawn for 1200 Greenwich Mean Time, the hour used as the prime time basis for construction of weather maps throughout the world. They were then typed in terms of the Cal-Tech method and classified for North America, Europe and the North Atlantic Ocean.

Meanwhile, if Dr. Millikan hoped that a more liberal outlook on Krick's long-range forecasting might be taking root in Washington now that its value had been demonstrated a number of times, he was disabused by a letter from Weather Bureau Chief Reichelderfer in mid-April 1943.

"I feel that specific forecasts beyond five or six days . . . may be misleading and are often inadvisable for military purposes, to say the least," Reichelderfer warned.

As the weeks passed, the Weather Bureau chief also fell to fretting about the operations of the peacetime associates Krick had left behind to keep his private weather service alive while he was in uniform. The income paid them a small livelihood and was used to carry on further research.

Reichelderfer wrote to Millikan twice about the matter, suggesting that he might want "to look into the present functioning of the so-called 'Research Council,' " as the group was called. Reichelderfer indicated that his chief concern was for the good name of CalTech.

The immediate cause of Reichelderfer's distress, it seemed, was that Krick's people had "knowingly" broken censorship regulations by getting weather information, "without proper authority," from a man who was also an observer for the weather bureau, on an unpaid basis. Millikan strongly objected to Reichelderfer's use of the word "knowingly," commenting that it was "just that kind of impugning of motives . . . that lies at the bottom of about nine-tenths of the difficulties that center about present forecasting procedures and situations."

Millikan went on to defend at great length the efforts of Krick and his group. His concern went beyond fending off the Weather Bureau's attacks. He also wanted to spread the word on what they were accomplishing, notably to the British, whose attitude in general toward long-range forecasting was much like that of the United States Weather Bureau.

In mid-July of 1943 Millikan saw an opportunity to speak of the subject to Field Marshall Sir John Dill, chief of the British Military

Mission to the United States, at a luncheon for Sir John and General Arnold in Washington. But he was suddenly called away from the table by a phone call.

In an immediate letter of apology to the distinguished Briton, Millikan wrote: "I had hoped to have a word with you about the development of American long-range forecasting with which our group at the California Institute of Technology has been intimately associated, and which might perhaps be of as much value to the British operations as General Arnold feels that it is being to the American Air Corps, as well as to other branches of the military service."

Millikan suggested, however, that Sir John could "get a good picture of the situation from your Mr. Hopkins of the British Central Scientific Office" in Washington. "Mr. Hopkins spent a day with us last week and gave me the impression that he was a man of very great grasp of all those related meteorological and radio problems which represent perhaps the most significant scientific advances in aid of the war which have been made in the past few years. I gained through him the impression that the British were not as conversant with the American activities in this field . . . as they might desire to be."

The British would soon be learning more—and would be as unreceptive as the U.S. Weather Bureau.

"Understand that you will go to England soon," General Arnold added in a handwritten postscript to a letter to Krick on October 10, 1943. "That will put you in a position where you can get a much better picture of our weather problems in connection with bombing than we have now—Good luck and see me upon your return. HHA."

6

I'll Slice as Thin as You Want

Arriving in England on temporary duty, Krick reported to General Ira Eaker at the Eighth Bomber Command. Eaker sent him to work with General Frederick L. Anderson, boss of the Eighth Air Force, whose headquarters were located underground outside London.

Krick soon learned what the problem was. The group's weatherman was simply giving the flight commanders bits of information— so many low clouds, so many high clouds, so many middle clouds— along the way to the target, over the target, and over the British Air Force bases. When the leader of a flight asked the weatherman for something more to the point, the weatherman hedged.

As a result, many missions were not getting off the ground. Approaching winter brought the promise of worse weather, and the Germans were gaining strength. General Anderson was getting restive. He was also becoming skeptical of the efficiency of his forecasting system. From time to time, as the weatherman continued to report targets socked in, he had sent a reconnaissance plane to take pictures of the area at target time—only to learn that the area was clear. Thus, many chances to hit the enemy were being lost for want of better weather forecasting.

"I want you to see if you can't cut these forecasts finer," Anderson told Krick.

"I'll slice them as thin as you want," Krick replied, "but you'll have a few aborted missions—we can't be perfect."

"We understand that," Anderson said. "Just tell us from your forecast—do we go or don't we. Better to abort a few missions than to keep sitting here on the ground while the krauts get stronger."

Krick replied, "Let's do it this way: You tell me what you need for the B-17 operations and what you need for the B-24s. [which could not fly as high as the B-17s]. Let me know what the specs are for the takeoff and return to base—route conditions for the fuel loads, target conditions—how many clouds you can stand, and the like. I'll put that blend into my mixer and come out with a yes or no—you can or you can't go."

Later, by the use of vertical glass plates spaced across a large map of Europe lying on a table, Krick depicted the weather in cross-section both vertically and horizontally, showing the pilots what lay ahead as well as below as they proceeded toward the target. Thus, applying an idea he had originated in Washington, Krick gave the airmen the "weather picture" in a literal sense, rather than relying on words alone, as was customary.

More bombs soon began falling on Europe. A target of special importance was a plant for making heavy water, operated by the Germans in connection with their atomic energy experiments. The plant lay hidden in one of the fjords of occupied Norway, nearly invisible except at high noon on a clear day.

The only time it was clear in Norway at that time of year— November—was when there was a big high pressure area over the country, feeding cold air clouds into the British bases and causing icing problems to aircraft as they took off or returned through these clouds.

Krick found a day when the cost in lost planes would be relatively low, and the heavy water plant was blown out of commission.

General Anderson became increasingly impressed with Krick's abilities, as did others of the Air Force high command in England. As the time neared for Krick's return to the United States, there was growing demand to keep him in Britain—or at least to get someone to take his place while he was home.

In the end, though, it was made clear that Krick himself was wanted back in England.

In Krick's pocket as he flew to Washington early in January, 1944, was a letter signed "Tooey" and stamped "Secret," from General Carl Spaatz, commander of the newly formed United States Strategic Air Forces in Europe, to his chief back home, General Arnold.

General Spaatz wanted something "absolutely essential" which the Strategic Air Forces had not had. This was a "coordinated weather forecasting system," including long-range forecasting. Except for Krick's work for the Eighth Bomber Command, Spaatz wrote, "there is no consistent long-range forecasting in this theater."

Spaatz intended to make up this lack, but he would need help since time was short. "The first step in this action has already been accomplished by the agreement of AAF Headquarters to release Colonel Krick for assignment," Spaatz wrote to Arnold. He mentioned a cable dated January 5, 1944.

He asked Arnold to help Krick get releases and orders for about ten men from the Weather Information Branch and have them as well as Krick "ordered over here at once on the highest priority." He added that Krick was expected to "be of invaluable assistance in forthcoming operations."

The operations General Spaatz had in mind were to rain bombs on Europe until Hitler had as little left as possible to hit back with when the Allies invaded France. The problem was to find suitable weather to carry out the bombing campaign code-named "Argument." The winter months over Europe historically were cloudy, hiding the targets and giving the enemy time to recover after each blow. The need was for a run of several good bombing days in a row.

With the hand-picked crew of forecasters General Spaatz wanted, Krick returned to England to find such a sequence of good bombing days. He was unaware that while he was in Washington his old nemesis, Dr. Rossby, as consultant to the War Department, had shown up in Britain and tried to block Krick's program, telling Spaatz that Krick had no scientific standing and would not be acceptable to the British, with whom the Americans had to coordinate operations.

Spaatz let it all go out the other ear and said nothing of the incident to Krick until the spring of 1944 after the air power he commanded, operating under Krick's weather forecasts, had gained superiority over the German Air Force and made rubble of key enemy targets.

The magic combination of days that made this possible took some time to discover. Searching between their briefings of bomber crews, Krick and Colonel Ben Holzman, who had earned his master's degree from Krick at CalTech, took turns at a grueling routine of thirty-six hours on and twelve hours off.

By early February, with D-Day coming up in June, there was still no such run of bombing weather in sight. Then Krick thought he saw what was needed taking shape: three days of clear weather. A high pressure area over Siberia was pushing westward across Germany, clearing out all cloudiness before it, but with snow along the forward edge. There had been a similar situation in 1928, as spotted by Krick and Holzman in searching their forty-year archive of classified hemispheric maps worked up earlier in the joint CalTech-New York University map project.

On February 17 Krick briefed General Spaatz and his deputy commander for operations, General Anderson, on what was coming.

"You can pull the string on the twentieth," Krick said. "There'll be three straight days of perfect weather—maybe a little more."

General Spaatz ordered the decks cleared for action—although, with the Germans at full defensive strength, he expected to lose as many as 250 planes on this first strike.

Krick disagreed. "The weather will be so lousy even when you take off, the fighters in Germany won't even be able to find you," he said.

Late on the night of February 19, with only hours to go, weathermen from the Eighth Air Force, now commanded by General James H. Doolittle, hero of the raid on Tokyo early in the war, reported it was still snowing at Leipzig, the main target. Doolittle canceled the strike.

"Sure, it will be snowing," pointed out Colonel Holzman, who had the duty that night, "but by the time you get there it will be clear."

General Spaatz thereupon countermanded the cancellation and rescheduled the takeoff for the early morning of February 20. Sure enough, when the bombers arrived over Germany it was snowing, and it kept snowing to within ten miles of Leipzig, just as forecast. Then the storm cleared, and Leipzig was left in flames. Hardly any fighters came up, the raiders not having been expected.

This was only a detail in the broader picture of what happened that morning to smash the Nazi war machine. All told, 11,000 men aboard 1,028 heavy bombers and 832 fighter planes were in the air over Germany, hitting key production centers. While General Doolittle and his Eighth Air Force struck from England, Major General Nathan F. Twining, commanding the Fifteenth Air Force, struck from Italy.

It was a good day. All but 25 Allied bombers and 4 fighters made it back to base. The Germans, swarming aloft to beat back the attackers where they were not caught unaware, as at Leipzig, lost 153 fighters.

Years later, as he walked one day in the Pentagon with his wife,

Marie, Krick would run into General Anderson, his old operations chief in England. Anderson threw his arms around Krick and said, "Doc, do you remember the day we won the war?" He meant that pivotal February day in 1944 when Leipzig was shattered, starting to turn the war around for the Allies.

For four more days the attack on Germany continued. When it finally ended, as bad weather returned, the German Air Force was badly crippled and never would recover its previous strength.

7

Operation Overload

Never in the history of war had there been anything like the invasion of Normandy—in scope, complexity, or the issue at stake.

Millions of men from many nations—land, sea and air forces—were coming by three thousand ships and fleets of airplanes that filled the skies, bringing with them several million tons of equipment. Their route was across the English Channel, their goal to land on the hostile shores of France and put an end to the rule of Adolf Hitler.

The weather in which to carry out this vast undertaking would have to meet certain complicated specifications. Otherwise, the Allied effort might fail. More than any other one factor, the weather held the key to success. For a number of days in advance there would have to be no winds that would raise a heavy, running swell in the Channel. The winds must be no more than nine-to-fourteen miles an hour in the Channel, or nineteen miles an hour outside it in open water.

The planes carrying troops and supplies needed a ceiling of at least 2500 feet and visibility of three miles. For the heavy bombers, the ceiling should be no lower than 11,000 feet, and the sky at least half-free of clouds below 5000 feet. Medium and light bombers called for a ceiling of 4500 feet minimum and visibility of no less than three miles over the target. For the fighter pilots there should be 1000 feet between the clouds and the ground.

Additionally, there was the problem of the paratroops. Twenty miles an hour was the most wind they could land in safely. The gliders, loaded with troops, could handle a thirty-five-mile wind, but no more. Both should have moonlight, twilight, or dawn, so they could see the earth without being seen too well themselves.

Once the crossing to Normandy had started and the landings begun, there could be no change of mind. The massive quantities of things needed to sustain the assaulting forces on the French coast must be kept coming—guns, ammunition, transport, tanks, food, medical supplies—600 to 700 tons a day for each division. At least five days of favorable weather would be needed to make the operation stick.

Moon, tide, and sunrise were right on June 5, 6, and 7, it was seen. "But the selection of the actual day would depend upon weather forecasts," General Dwight D. Eisenhower, the commander of the invasion, wrote in *Crusade In Europe*, "If none of the three days should prove satisfactory from the standpoint of weather, consequences would ensue that were almost terrifying to contemplate.

"Secrecy would be lost. Assault troops would be unloaded and crowded back into assembly areas enclosed in barbed wire, where their original places would already have been taken by those to follow in subsequent waves. Complicated movement tables would be scrapped. Morale would drop. A wait of at least 14 days, possibly 28, would be necessary—a sort of suspended animation involving more than 2,000,000 men!"

So the burden rested on the backs of the weathermen, in particular on Colonels Krick and Holzman. Working with them were four British, two from the Air Ministry and two from the Admiralty; neither pair had much use for the kind of forecasting the Americans were doing. The presiding British forecaster had said scornfully months before, when Krick first came to London, that a five-day forecast was out of the question. His views on long-range forecasting had survived unaffected by Krick's and Holzman's work for the USSTAF bombing campaign in February.

Making matters no easier was the touch-and-go character of the weather over the North Atlantic and Western Europe at the start of June, showing the usual fitfulness of seasonal change from spring to summer. The British, staying with their traditional short-range forecasts, could see nothing ahead to encourage the launching of history's greatest water-borne invasion.

Using analogues (a previous weather sequence that resembles the current weather chart and immediately before it) selected from their archive, Krick and Holzman saw possibilities. They also saw that, in any event, the weather was going to get no better as June grew older. The first days of the month offered "possible" days, those later, when the tide again would be right, "impossible."

As events came down to the wire, with June 4 picked as the first date, June 5 and 6 as alternates, the arguments among the weathermen grew louder. Several times each day they got together by scrambler telephone from their separate stations in what was loosely called a conference, to talk about how things looked for the next five days: winds, clouds, rain, visibility, condition of sea and surf. The consensus—when there was one—was used by the weather briefing officer at General Eisenhower's headquarters in Portsmouth to advise the supreme commander on emerging weather developments. Group-Captain James M. Stagg performed this function.

The wrangling on the phones became so spirited that Krick and Holzman kept a diary on each day's discussion, taking turns dictating what was said. Beginning on June 2, here is something of how it went, told from the secret record:

"At the 0730 Conference, Widewing [code name for USSTAF,

Krick's outfit] indicated no change in their forecasts. . . . Admiralty leaned a bit toward the ETA [Air Ministry] picture so Group-Captain Stagg threw out the Widewing version which was optimistic and prepared a summary based largely upon the ETA-Admiralty picture. . . . Dr. Sutcliff [at Allied Fighter Command, an occasional participant in the discussion] indicated that the forecast, as prepared by Group-Captain Stagg, as far as he was concerned, "was not worth a damn. . . ."

Differences did not improve as the day advanced. At five o'clock in the afternoon, a conference was called from Eisenhower's headquarters by Colonel Yates of USSTAF, who had gone to Portsmouth to help Group-Captain Stagg keep Ike informed. As at the earlier confab, "the ETA continued to throw a note of pessimism in the forecast," with Dr. Petterssen saying "the situation was a treacherous one." The Admiralty agreed with the dark view taken by the Air Ministry, as before.

Krick and Holzman, however, "continued to offer an optimistic picture."

It was the same with Krick and Holzman at eight o'clock. Holzman, who led the discussion, said that "every indication corroborated an optimistic viewpoint." Dr. Petterssen, on the other hand, "came on and reiterated his stand that the situation warranted no optimism whatsoever."

The two sides were still at odds with each other next morning at the six o'clock conference. If anything, they seemed to have dug in a little deeper in their respective positions during the night. "Every indication pointed to a very optimistic viewpoint for the entire forecast period," Colonel Holzman emphasized, while Petterssen, for his part, "took an alarmingly pessimistic view, the Air Ministry going along with him. All was gloom."

Krick and Holzman stood fast. At the next conference of the day, a couple of hours later, they "steadfastly maintained their position on the forecast, which continued to develop exactly as anticipated." This upset Colonel Yates, who complained that Krick and Holzman were placing him in an embarrassing light.

At the war room briefing of 4:15 in the afternoon of June 3, Krick presented the forecast for the next five days. It indicated operational weather for both sea and air forces, beginning after the next day. The British saw it exactly the other way around: weather unfit for either plane or ship throughout the same five days.

The reason for Krick and Holzman's stubborn optimism was a "wedge development" or high-pressure belt over the Atlantic which they expected to reach the British Isles on June 4, pushing a cold front ahead of it into France and bringing clearing weather in its wake. The wedge had not yet shown up on the daily weather charts, however, so Krick and Holzman decided it was useless to argue and accepted the majority opinion.

Also, this brought a fleeting measure of peace to Colonel Yates down at Portsmouth, who had phoned Krick and Holzman that it would make his job a lot easier if they would agree with the others. Yates didn't say so, but the strain had become too much for Group-Captain Stagg, who had collapsed, leaving Yates to carry the whole load. Nor did it help Yates that the Russians were sending Eisenhower cables advising him not to go.

But at the first conference on June 4, at three o'clock in the morning, with the Admiralty now saying that the outlook was even blacker than they at first thought, Krick and Holzman fought for their views.

"Colonel Krick presented in great detail the Widewing viewpoint in order that the reasons for our optimistic position would be made perfectly clear to the other members of the conference," Holzman wrote in his notes of the meeting. "Our final statement was that we were in fair agreement with the wind forecast for Sunday (the day now begun), but not the cloud forecast for that day, and that beyond Sunday we had no confidence whatever in the conference forecast (which was for all bad weather)."

But it was no use. The conference forecast prevailed, and the invasion of Normandy was canceled for both Sunday and Monday, June 4 and June 5.

So matters stood through the day until the five o'clock discussion in the afternoon. Suddenly the British wavered. The Admiralty now said it favored Krick and Holzman's picture over that of the Air Ministry, which went on seeing the worst, including fog on June 6 over the beaches in Normandy.

When all again talked things over, at three o'clock in the morning of June 5, Dr. Petterssen began to retreat from his position, indicating he was no longer sure of his pessimistic stand. The Admiralty, which had wavered the day before, wavered some more, saying that "developments seemed to be going somewhat better than they had hoped for." Krick and Holzman "continued to reiterate their optimistic picture."

The conference ended, one of them recorded, "with the implication that the operation [invasion] was on."

Indeed, it was. As the attack unfolded on June 6 without interference from the weather, the generals congratulated Colonels Krick and Holzman for sticking with their forecast despite the disagreement of the others. "If the forecast holds up as you have indicated," said General Edward Curtis, General Spaatz' deputy, "it will make history."

There was something else besides Krick and Holzman's unyielding optimism that the weather would hold which helped the great decision along. On Sunday night, June 4, when the final decision had to be made, and unknown to Krick and Holzman, General Spaatz had called on General Eisenhower. "I think you should go," Spaatz said. "Our guys know what they're talking about."

With grim humor as the invasion rolled on, General Curtis sought out Krick and said, "We'll all be busted to privates if you two guys are wrong."

Not years alone have turned Krick's hair from jet black to snow white.

With a hold on Europe solidly established, General Eisenhower removed the British from all forecasting functions and assigned this responsibility exclusively to the forecasters of the United States Strategic Air Forces. He elevated Krick to chief of his weather information section, in due course stationed at his forward headquarters at Rheims, forecasting for all operations in the re-conquest of the continent.

Air Marshal Tedder of the Royal Air Force, Eisenhower's chief deputy, was briefed daily by Krick and Holzman. He grew so confident of the pair's ability that he telephoned Krick's headquarters for the weather each time he was in England, ready to fly back to France, ignoring the forecasts of his own British Air Ministry weathermen at RAF stations.

Long-range forecasting as developed at the California Institute of Technology brought one other major benefit to the course of the war. The Allies needed to know the earliest possible time when they could cross the Rhine into Germany with the least chance of being cut off from their supplies by the frequent spring flooding of the river from rain and melting snow high in the Alps. The historical record, as established by a group of engineers and flood control experts sent over from the United States, showed that the Rhine could flood any time until May 1.

Krick determined that the winter of 1944–45 likely would be very dry and cold for all of northern Europe. The Rhine would almost certainly be safe from any floods. He handed this information to General Eisenhower's G-2 Chief in January. It placed the odds on crossing the Rhine early in the season without danger of flood at about 92 percent.

Plans were speeded up and the crossing of the Rhine started on March 7. Two months later the war suddenly was over—about the time the Allies were supposed to be still poised on the west bank of the Rhine. Thus at least a part of Germany had been saved for occupation by the Western powers rather than the Soviet Union.

8

Somebody Else Will Need
What You've Got

For "exceptionally meritorious conduct in the performance of out-standing services" during the war—namely, the application of long-range weather forecasting to the uses of battle, Krick was awarded the Bronze Star with Oak Leaf Cluster, the Legion of Merit, and France's *croix de guerre avec étoile de vermeille*.

But apart from these kudos, the prophet classically found little honor in his home country, save from those who knew him best. These liked his idea for extending worldwide the benefits of long-range weather forecasting for the needs of peace, as it had been made to serve in war.

Krick wrote of his plan to his old friend, Dr. Robert A. Millikan at the California Institute of Technology, asking for a reinstatement of his credentials at the school and for an extension of the leave of absence which General Arnold had obtained for him at the outset of war.

Dr. Millikan responded with enthusiasm. "In view of your

71

large experience in forecasting for the D-Day invasion and the other weather services connected with the AAF in the European theater and elsewhere," Millikan wrote on June 5, 1945, "it would be useful for you before returning to the Institute to make contacts with the European meteorologists who, like yourself, are interested in the improvement of long-range weather forecasts, particularly in view of the fact that you inform me that you find that French, Russian and other European meteorologists have been approaching the long-range forecasting problem with techniques very similar to those which you yourself have developed."

Krick also wrote General Arnold about his plan. He pointed out that only private forecasters were able to provide an international weather service because public weather services had trouble operating outside their own countries.

Hearing more about the plan directly from Krick when the two met in Washington soon afterward, Arnold exclaimed, "I'll buy that!" He brought in Colonel Yates and General Hoyt S. Vandenberg, his assistant chief of staff, and had Krick tell them what he had in mind. Arnold instructed Yates to set up what was needed at the Washington end while Krick headed overseas, taking along several letters of introduction from Arnold to officials in South America, including the chief of staff of the Brazilian Air Force.

Arnold liked the idea that when he turned the wartime Air Transport Command over to commercial operators, they would have access to Krick's long-range weather service around the world. He called Krick's plan "of tremendous importance to the United States."

But Krick had failed to reckon with the United States Weather Bureau. At a meeting of the Provisional International Air Transport Association, the Weather Bureau was instrumental in getting a resolution passed which barred the airlines from using any part of their airmail subsidy to pay for private weather service. Bureau Chief Reichelderfer personally had the scheme killed in Brazil by writing to his counterpart in that country.

72

American carriers, in other words, would have to go on using the Weather Bureaus within the countries they served. They could not hire Irving Krick, here or anywhere else in the world.

Krick returned to CalTech to resume the work he had left for the war, bringing with him a group of British trainees from an international consultant service he had formed in England, sponsored by J. Arthur Rank, the film magnate. At CalTech, Krick planned to set up an international training center in the techniques of long-range forecasting. Then, in 1947, Dr. Millikan retired and was succeeded by Dr. Lee DuBridge, who for several years had been director of the radiation laboratory at MIT, Professor Rossby's former school.

One of Dr. DuBridge's first actions was to get rid of CalTech's meteorology department—and Irving Krick.

This all came as small surprise to Dr. Millikan, who had told Krick, "You'll never get anywhere with this fellow. My advice is to leave here. Take your staff with you. Find a way to carry on with your work of investigating atmospheric behavior, applying as you go what you find out—as we've always done."

Von Karman advised the same course. "With this new administration there's no future for you at CalTech."

Krick wanted to see another old friend. In his own little plane he and his new British bride, Marie, flew up to Sonora, California, and had a visit with General Arnold at the veteran soldier's ranch. As the pair walked in the garden, Arnold put his arm around Krick's shoulders and said, "Doc, I want you to continue your investigations because there'll come a time when somebody else will need what you've got. I'm not in Washington anymore, but they can still hear my bark. I'll see to it that you get support while you're getting on your feet."

Setting up for business in Pasadena, Krick and his group received a substantial contract from the Air Force and settled down to a resumption of their long-range forecasting service and studies—

until General Arnold died. The contract with the Air Force was canceled next day.

In 1949, the Weather Bureau took steps to shoot down *all* private weather forecasters, a technique that promised to get Krick without making it appear they were especially aiming at him. The Bureau caused legislation to be introduced in Congress which would allow it to take over the specialized services of the private practitioners.

This action raised the hackles of the American Legion, which angrily accused the Weather Bureau of using "devious means and methods" to drive out of business these weather experts who at war's end had been urged to "carry on in the science of applied meteorology on a private, civilian basis, so that in the event of another emergency our country would have the vital ready reservoir of professionally competent and experienced meteorologists to man the defense . . ."

The Legionnaires recalled that, in response to protests from the private forecasters, the Bureau had promised to let up on them. The Bureau thereupon had adopted a "six-point program which was read into the Congressional Record, and which was subscribed to by the United States Weather Bureau as the policy to which they would honorably adhere thereafter in regard to these ex-GI private meteorologists."

At its annual convention in 1949 the Legion called on Congress to make a law out of the Weather Bureau's sig-point program of behavior toward private weathermen. The Bureau forestalled this action by naming a "coordinator" to work with the private operators. No law was needed, it maintained.

At this time Krick was experimenting with something new, making the Weather Bureau unhappy with him all over again. This was artificial nucleation of the clouds to increase rain and snow. At Schenectady, New York, Dr. Irving Langmuir, Nobel laureate in chemistry in 1932 and director of General Electric's research laboratories, along with Vincent Schaefer, had discovered the principle of "cloud seeding," in July, 1946.

Dr. Irving P. Krick studying incoming teletype and facsimile data at his headquarters.

Jimmie James in 1930 climbing into a Douglas M-2 mail plane. As chief pilot and vice president of operations for Western Air Express, forerunner of Western Airlines, he gave young Irving Krick his first break as a long range weather forecaster. (Courtesy Western Airlines)

Pilots of the early days at Western Air Express who trusted Krick's forecasts. In front of a Douglas M-2 mail plane are (left to right) pilots Fred Kelly, Jimmy James, Al DeGarmo, Maurice Graham, and operations manager Corliss C. Moseley. (Courtesy Western Airlines)

American bombers, benefitting from long range weather forecasting, rain destruction on Germany in World War II. (National Archives)

Krick and fellow officers picked the best probable weather conditions for the invasion of North Africa. Here American troops go ashore in landing craft near Casablanca. (National Archives)

Americans landing on the Normandy beaches on D-Day. The timing was crucial, and this was the greatest triumph of long range weather forecasting during the war. (National Archives)

Home on leave from duty in Europe, Krick visited Spencer Tracy at an MGM studio in Hollywood.

Krick explaining the rudiments of meteorology to members of the original Mickey Mouse Club during filming at Walt Disney Studios in 1956.

Cloud seeding operations in a moving storm: The ground generator projects silver iodide particles into the atmosphere at the rate of about one quadrillion per minute. The particles are carried into the clouds and diffused by natural turbulence and updrafts. Within the cloud each particle becomes a potential snowflake at temperatures near 20 degrees Fahrenheit or lower. This illustration, reproduced here, was included in a paper Krick presented before the Royal Society of Arts in London in 1954.

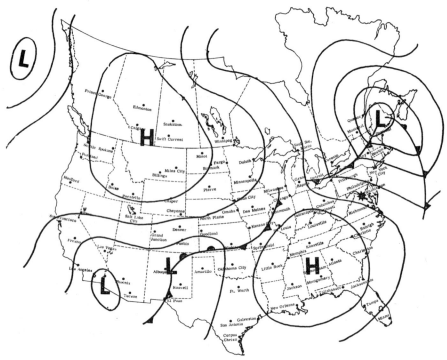

KRICK'S FORECAST
JANUARY 20, 1977
PREPARED : APRIL 1972

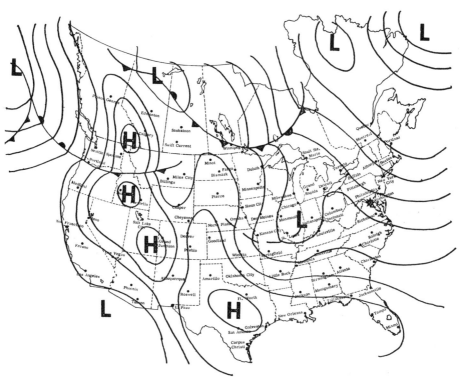

ACTUAL WEATHER MAP 1200Z
JANUARY 20,1977

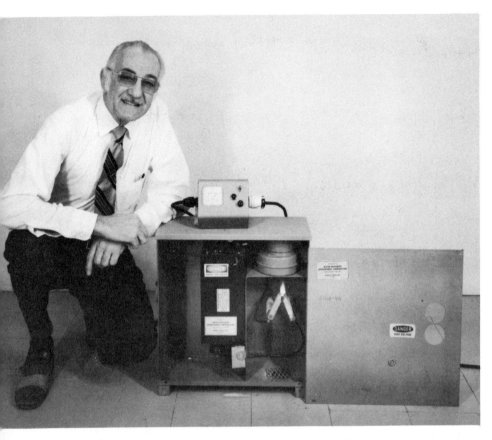

George Orlich with Krick patented the silver iodide arc type generator for ground dispersal of silver iodide. A typical generator is shown here.

Close-up of a silver iodide arc type generator. Solid silver iodide rods (electrodes) are eroded at the rate of two grams per hour by this unit. The control box here shown on top usually is located in the operator's house nearby while the unit itself is located outside. It is activiated on a call from Krick headquarters in Palm Springs, California, as an evolving weather situation dictates.

Krick describes various cloudseeding projects operating in the United States.

What they found had to do with a central secret of nature, that every raindrop and snowflake has a nucleus. These nuclei come from countless sources: the soil, vegetation, salt spray from the oceans, smokestacks, automobile exhaust pipes, aircraft emissions. Some particles form on their own by chemical reaction in the atmosphere. "Condensation, or ice, nuclei," weathermen call them because they attract water, just as surface objects under the right conditions attract dew.

When several million moisture molecules have collected like swarming bees on a speck of nuclei, they form a droplet, or ice crystal, depending upon the temperatures within the clouds where the process begins. When many million droplets come together, they make a raindrop or, in the case of ice crystals, a snowflake.

If the cloud is "super-cooled" no ice crystals form, no matter how abundant the ice nuclei in nature, because of the peculiar behavior characteristics of those nuclei. Nothing may happen until the temperature of the cloud gets down to about five degrees above zero. At that point ice nuclei from certain soils may initiate the formation of ice crystals. The cloud—in summer usually a cumulus —mushrooms upward like an atomic explosion.

Inside the cloud, meanwhile, the ice crystals go on attracting moisture, growing rapidly larger. In ten to twenty minutes, as gravity takes over, the fatted ice crystals are on their way to earth as snow-flakes, growing larger still as they encounter yet more droplets on the way down. They reach the ground as snow if the temperature is freezing or rain if it's above freezing.

Nature's work of building ice crystals into snowflakes improves as the cloud grows higher and colder. The process works best at about 13° below zero. But if there aren't enough bits of dust in the rising air, not much of anything happens: there's no rain, no snow. Without the "seeds," or ice nuclei, no ice crystals form, regardless of the temperature.

There is a point on the thermometer, however, at which the droplets give up and finally turn into ice crystals on their own, without the help of nuclei. This point is roughly 40° below zero.

And this "flashover" is unanimous. No droplets are left to make rain or snow—it's all ice, ornamenting the heavens with the graceful brush strokes and mare's-tails of high-flying cirrus clouds.

So, clearly, nature's methods for getting the water back to earth, once the sun has pulled it up from the oceans and elsewhere, is not as efficient as it might be. Studies of thunderstorms in the eastern United States indicate that only about 5 percent of the water overhead ever makes it to the ground. In the dryer areas of the country, like the Great Plains, the clouds are usually so high up that what rain does start to earth sometimes disappears on the way. Scientists estimate that the "rivers" that flow by overhead carry six times as much water as those on the surface.

What Langmuir and his colleagues discovered was that these sky rivers can be made to yield more water by introducing artificial ice nuclei into the atmosphere. On these, snowflakes will form at much warmer temperatures than on those ice nuclei available in nature.

After much experimentation, it was found that the best seeding material was silver iodide, discovered by Bernard Vonnegut, likewise of GE's research staff. It was found to have nearly the same crystal structure as the ice crystal. Vaporized, silver iodide yields about 600,000 billion particles per gram—the amount you can put on your fingernail—each a potential snowflake or raindrop.

Besides being highly diffusive, with one gram filling several cubic miles of sky, silver iodide takes effect sooner than nature's own nuclei. It goes to work at around 25° down in the lower, more moist cloud layers rather than holding off until it is much colder. Since that is the temperature where most of the water is—sometimes three-quarters of the cloud—silver iodide clearly improves on nature's own seeds as a rainmaker.

This knowledge of how to woo the clouds for more rain came to light bit by bit as Krick joined the investigation and began experimenting with artificial nucleation during the winter of 1946–1947, a few months after Langmuir announced what he and Schaefer had learned at Schenectady.

90

Working with CalTech graduate students under his direction, Krick at first tried dry ice as the nucleating agent, heaving it into the clouds from an airplane. This was the material Langmuir had first used, silver iodide not being found to be useful until later. Gradually Krick became convinced that this method of modifying the clouds was inherently faulty. For one thing, when it was good seeding weather it was often poor flying weather. Also, the seeding that could be done from an airplane was relatively local in scope, while nature's storm processes operated on a vastly greater scale.

Krick turned his attention to finding a way to do the seeding from the ground. He developed a generator, or small furnace, which, after further research and experimentation with fuels and chemicals and trying it all out in assorted weather, released silver iodide crystals, or ice-forming nuclei, in what seemed to be the best size and number, into the rising currents typically present when the seeding time is right. Such a time occurs only when conditions are correct for nature's own rather inefficient rain process.

Using his ground generators, Krick went on experimenting for a couple more years, working in southern California and near Phoenix, Arizona. He then accepted an invitation to visit Langmuir, who had gone on with his own experiments, to compare notes and discuss the possibility of working together.

"I think it would be wise to plan for you to come to Schenectady and spend a day or two talking over the results that we have had," Langmuir wrote Krick on February 25, 1949. "Then we . . . might go to Arizona or Pasadena and look over and discuss the results that you have obtained. After that, we may find that it is desirable to make recommendations in regard to some joint operations."

But other visitors had preceded Krick to Schenectady, and he was unprepared for Langmuir's greeting. "What is this with you and the Weather Bureau?" Langmuir asked curiously. "They came up here and just really emasculated you to me. They told me you were a nut—you're unscientific—don't know what you're doing, and so on and on."

Since Langmuir was working under GE contracts on a project for the Army, Navy and Air Force, he prudently found reasons to go on alone, without Krick. He advised Krick, however, to continue with his plans for commercial seeding operations.

By early 1950 Krick was ready to start putting his rainmaking knowledge and equipment to useful purpose on a wide scale. His action was in line with Dr. Millikan's philosophy, enunciated years before, that as learning was acquired in the classroom and laboratory, it should be applied in the field. Krick formed the Water Resources Development Corporation, with headquarters in Pasadena, and his first commercial customer was a wheat grower, Leo Horrigan, in the Horse Heaven area of eastern Washington. Horrigan was in danger of losing his crop from drought in June and came to Krick to see what might be done to save it.

The story of how it rained after Krick seeded the clouds over Horrigan's 100,000 acres and brought him a fine harvest that summer, while it stayed dry all around his land, traveled far and fast. It resulted in a phone call from Tom Dines, a banker in Denver, who knew of Krick's work during the war.

"I just found out that one of my directors is a big cattleman in New Mexico," Dines told Krick. "His name is Albert Mitchell. I suggested to him that maybe cloud-seeding would improve his rangelands so he could carry more cattle on them. I told him about you and what you're doing."

Albert Mitchell joined with some of his neighbors to hire Krick. A month after he completed his seeding program for Horrigan in Washington, Krick had a cloud-seeding project underway for Mitchell which continued intermittently for the next twenty-one years.

Krick extended his operations throughout the West during the growing drought of the early 1950s and moved to Denver, seeding the clouds not only to bring rain to crops, but to improve stream flows as well, including that of the Columbia River, chief source of power in the Pacific Northwest, where an approaching dry spell brought the threat of brownouts.

92

The Columbia River project grew out of Krick's earlier work with the Salt River Project in Arizona. Dick Searles, president of the Salt River Project, had become Secretary of the Interior under President Truman and one summer day in 1951 he phoned Krick at his Denver office.

"Go up to the Bonneville power administration and make a contract with them to seed the Columbia River basin," Searles directed. "Let's see if we can't get some more water in the river by fall."

In a matter of weeks, with heavy rains in September during Krick's seeding operations, the Columbia River had risen to the point that the job was considered done. The Bureau of Reclamation, establishing a historical relationship between a gauging station on the Columbia in Montana and another on the Kootenay River in Canada, found that the flow of the Columbia had increased 83 percent above what might have been expected.

The Bureau of Reclamation came to this conclusion over the objections of Weather Bureau statisticians who took part in the evaluation and said that the finding was meaningless.

Krick soon was applying his cloud-seeding techniques to a larger area than anyone else being mentioned in the scientific journals of the time—more than 150 million acres—and was refining his methods as he proceeded. One project alone covered more than 30,000 square miles.

Wherever he appeared, invited by farmers, ranchers and water officials to tell them what he might be able to do to bring them rain, Krick found that he was not totally among strangers; his Weather Bureau "friends" were in the audience, alert to warn his hosts that there was nothing he could do to help them—that he was a faker.

"They followed me like fleas," Krick once remarked.

When the farmers got together and formed what they called the National Weather Improvement Association, holding their first convention in Denver, with Krick as the featured speaker, they were soon aware of an uninvited guest in their midst. "Be careful about this fellow," warned the Weather Bureau's emissary as he circulated among them. "He doesn't know what he's doing. There's nothing to cloud seeding. The government doesn't believe in it or we would be doing it for you for nothing."

A single doubter in a group considering Krick's rainmaking services was often enough to make them scatter like quail and forget the whole thing.

As the Weather Bureau continued to dog his steps, his clients became fewer and fewer. About the only groups who stayed with him were those that included engineers—such as power companies and municipal water supply officials—who could assess things for themselves.

The Weather Bureau seemed never to let up on its determination to drive Krick out of business.

"I have received a clipping from the Denver *Post* . . . which contains a picture and description of a weather forecast display in the U. S. National Bank in Denver," wrote Bureau Chief Reichelderfer one day in 1951. Reichelderfer quoted the words under the offending photograph:

Seven-day weather forecasts and past weather records for the current month are now available to customers of the United States National Bank in Denver. Here Yvonne Robertson of the bank's personnel department puts one of the forecasts in the bank's window. The display contains two forecasts, covering the eastern and western slopes, as an added service to ski fans and others in Denver who want to know western slope weather. The forecasts are prepared by Dr. Irving P. Krick, meteorological consultant.

"Of course, I would not question the propriety of furnishing forecasts from your Denver office to the bank," Reichelderfer went on, "but in this case it seems that unless the newspaper description is in error, the public display is not in accordance with the terms of the teletype license, paragraph 2, which provides that the licensee shall not use any of the reports or information for any purpose except that of providing a private consultant meteorological service of a specialized and individual nature."

Reichelderfer said he thought Krick would like to look into the matter and said he would appreciate knowing what he found out.

Mindful that the subject had been considered important enough to engage the personal attention of the top man in the Bureau, Krick rose to the crisis without delay.

"This matter was reviewed by our legal department . . . and since the display does not in any way violate our agreement to refrain from publishing forecasts in newspapers or over the radio," he reported to Reichelderfer, "the opinion rendered to us indicated that the Bank was on sound ground since the material is for the benefit of their clients and not for the general public."

The Bureau was not mollified. Shortly there arrived a new communication, this one from I. R. Tannehill, chief of the Synoptic Reports and Forecasts Division, who was acting during Reichelderfer's absence in Europe.

"It seems to me that publication in the meaning intended in the basic license, coupled with the phrase, 'or for any purpose except that of providing a private consultant meteorological service of a specialized and individual nature,' clearly excludes forms of publication in the broad sense, whether newspapers, radio, window display, or any other method which reaches the *general* public or any part thereof which does not in fact consist of clients of the licensee," Tannehill argued.

The passerby on the sidewalk, he went on, wasn't entitled to see the information in the window. "Removal of the display to the interior is a step in the right direction," he concluded.

Krick patiently endured the Weather Bureau's bedevilments, but by the autumn of 1951 it was time to draw the line—with the line being drawn by Krick's lawyer, T. R. Gillenwaters, who wrote Reichelderfer:

"I have had called to my attention a clipping from the Scottsbluff, Nebraska *Star Herald* newspaper, in which your E. L. Van Tassel, the Scottsbluff weather observer, is quoted at length on other items than those that appear to me to be related to his duties as a weather observer and which directly affect our organization."

Some of Van Tassel's remarks had made the ranchers feel that the Weather Bureau was meddling in their business—"when they might better be spending their time improving the weather service," Gillenwaters wrote.

"The statement that 'a generator can be built by a blacksmith for approximately $50,' and that 'the daily consumption of silver iodide is estimated at 10¢ per machine day' is, of course, obviously intended to cast aspersions upon our organization, as we are engaged in a project for increasing rainfall in the area adjacent to Scottsbluff."

Gillenwaters said he had been getting the same kind of reports from Arizona, Oklahoma, Texas, Kansas, and Montana—reports of Weather Bureau men bad-mouthing not only Krick but anyone else doing cloud-seeding. If it kept up, he threatened to sue the Weather Bureau.

Reichelderfer in reply accused Gillenwaters of wanting to gag the Weather Bureau on the topic of rainmaking, saying such "an approach does not make it any easier to bring about the cooperation and constructive planning espoused by your letter." He said the position of the Bureau was that it didn't know if cloud-seeding worked or not, but was "very eager to get the facts," including any information the Krick organization might have.

In September, 1952, Krick gained moral support from a group of United States senators who had lost patience with the Weather Bureau for its negative approach to cloud-seeding. The senators were all from states in want of rain. At a joint hearing of three subcommittees on legislation to do something about the drought, they accused the Bureau of trying to prove that cloud-seeding was a failure instead of trying to develop a technique to help the farmers. They accused it of having a closed mind and of being against anyone with an idea that threatened change.

The senatorial storm hit when Willard F. McDonald, the bulky, gray-haired assistant chief of the Weather Bureau, started to justify the Bureau's conservatism. He was cut off by Senator Clinton Anderson of New Mexico, chairman of the meeting, who roared, "You have consistently fought artificial rainmaking!"

McDonald replied defensively that, on the contrary, the Weather Bureau had conducted numerous experiments to produce rain, using both dry ice and silver iodide, but still wasn't ready to say that any rain that followed wouldn't have fallen anyhow.

"The Bureau feels," said McDonald, "that it is still too early to try to define what can or cannot be done in this field and that a great deal more work is necessary before sound conclusions can be formed."

Senator Francis Case of South Dakota said that ranchers in his state had paid a professional rainmaker to seed clouds on twenty successive Fridays and that on twenty successive Saturdays it rained. "Are you not willing to concede that this proves the efficacy of cloud seeding?" Case demanded.

McDonald was not. "That," he retorted, "is like saying that if a bunch of women hang out their washings on Monday, and it rains Wednesday, the rain is caused by hanging out the washings."

That at least left everybody laughing.

Krick persevered, and in late 1953 he signed the first of two contracts with Oklahoma City to seed the clouds for rain. By what followed, he won a sturdy partisan to his side in the person of Morrison B. Cunningham, superintendent and engineer of the Oklahoma City Water Department, who later became the city's director of public works.

"We had a contract with Dr. Krick last year which saved our life," Cunningham wrote to Robert S. Millar of the Denver Water Board, "and we got from 75 percent to 100 percent normal precipitation in the target area of our watershed, and it looks as if we would have received only 50 percent without his help."

In a similar optimistic vein, Cunningham wrote to a dozen or so other quarters where there might be interest in hearing about

Krick—the *Farm Journal*, the Associated Press, county agents, city water departments, colleges, universities. . . . "During the term of Dr. Krick's contract, the river changed from a dry to a flowing stream," more than doubling the flow over the previous year, Cunningham wrote.

"We have more water in our reservoirs this year than for two years and the river valley is in the best condition to receive a flow of water with a minimum of losses than in the past two years. I am convinced that cloud-seeding, when conducted by experienced people like Dr. Krick's organization, we can assume is to be a new scientific approach to increasing precipitation."

But by this time, despite the missionary work of Morrison Cunningham, Krick was barely hanging on. The Weather Bureau had been reaching a far larger audience. He cut his staff from seventy to a handful and was wondering what to do next when he ran into a longtime friend, industrialist Floyd Odlum, whose wife, Jackie Cochrane, always depended on Krick for weather forecasts before taking off on any of her flying exploits.

Odlum wanted to make some investments in Spain, and it struck him that it might be interesting to convince the nation's dictator, Francisco Franco, to give him a concession to make rain in Spain. Krick thus became rainmaker for the Spanish government, seeding the clouds to bring down extra water for the Ministries of Air and Agriculture as well as for private power companies, which wanted more water in the rivers and reservoirs.

For Union Electrica Madrilena, Krick took the job on a contingency basis: that he be paid for each specified increment the river rose in a relation established between that river and some adjacent rainfall or river gauging stations. If there was no rise in the river, he would get no pay. After two years, the Spaniards were paying Odlum so much money for Krick's work that they asked to change the deal to a flat-fee basis. The reservoir was up about 70 percent above expectancy, based on the formula developed by the client.

Then the French, hearing what the Yankee rainmaker was doing below the Pyrenees, became interested. After sending engineers from Electricité de France, headed by the President of the French Meteorological Society, to Spain to see firsthand what was going on, they engaged Krick to lay down rain and snow to raise the water level of an important reservoir high in the French Alps. The area was also a first-class ski resort, which could benefit from the project.

The French Meteorological Society reported the results. "For the first winter (1954–55), significant increase of 42.3 percent. For the second winter (1955–56), 78 percent; for each total year taken individually, 1954–55, 26.5 percent; 1955–56, 19 percent; for the series of two consecutive years, 1954–56, 23.7 percent."

This showing, the society commented, was "doubtless due to the excellent natural location of the watershed and the competence of the operating company, which was Water Resources Development Corporation, of Denver, Colorado."

Whereupon Krick was elected an honorary member of the French Meteorological Society.

In New York, Mary Lasker, a friend of Floyd Odlum and prominent in Hadassah, contracted with Krick to go to Israel for three years on a rainmaking mission there. "Can you grow wheat in the Negev?" Prime Minister Ben Gurion asked, referring to the desert near Beersheba.

"The rainfall characteristics there are similar to those in our eastern Washington-Oregon area and we're doing well there," Krick answered, "Yes, I think we can grow wheat in the Negev."

A photograph taken in the Negev a year later by Krick showed his project director, Lewis O. Grant, standing in wheat up to his chest.

In Italy the city of Genoa was building aqueducts to bring more water to the city's reservoirs which it wanted to be kept brimful while construction was in progress. They called on Krick. When he had accommodated the Genoese and returned home, former

President Segne of Italy wrote to him, in effect, "Dams and reservoirs have been built in Sardinia under the Marshall Plan of your country. The reservoirs are supposed to be used to develop power and provide irrigation for agriculture, but they have no water in them. Will you come and bring us some rain to fill them?"

Krick did, working from 1958 to 1961.

None of Krick's cloud-seeding successes overseas appeared to impress the U. S. Weather Bureau, however. It kept after him—wherever he might be. While he was in Israel, the head of the Bureau's research division, Dr. Harry Wexler, wrote to the chief of Israel's weather bureau seeking to discredit Krick—though wheat grew in the Negev and Israelis trained by Krick helped to carry on his cloud-seeding project after he left. Wexler, while on duty with the U. S. Army Air Forces during the war, had scorned Krick's methods.

In time the Bureau of Reclamation joined with the Weather Bureau in tracking Krick. Repeatedly its representatives arrived on the scene, injecting controversy and confusion into a discussion as Krick negotiated a cloud-seeding contract—in Lebanon, South Africa, and elsewhere. This generally put an end to the proceedings.

9

Does It Bring Rain
Or Doesn't It?

In 1953 steps were taken to settle, once and for all, the question of whether or not cloud-seeding worked. The father of this enterprise was New Mexico's Albert K. Mitchell, who had looked up Krick in 1950 after learning about him from Denver banker Tom Dines. Thanks to timely rains that followed seeding of the clouds by Krick, Mitchell had just put up the biggest hay crop he had harvested in years.

Mitchell was a personal friend of Dwight Eisenhower, who had been elected President, and he suggested to Eisenhower—as well as to Senator Clinton Anderson of New Mexico—that a committee be formed to make a survey of all the cloud-seeding that had been going on, by professionals and amateurs alike, and see how it came out. Did it bring rain and, if so, how much?

Senator Francis Case of South Dakota, himself involved in cloud-seeding experiments, introduced a bill to create the President's Advisory Committee on Weather Control to be composed of five members from the fields of science, agriculture, and business and six from appropriate government departments and agencies.

Passed by Congress, the bill was signed into law by the President on August 13, 1953. On December 9, the President named the members, and on December 18, the committee's chairman, Captain Harold T. Orville, who had been the Navy's head weatherman during the war, charting the weather for Jimmie Doolittle's famous raid on Tokyo, convened the first meeting of the group.

Its job, as Captain Orville spelled it out, was to "study and evaluate public and private experiments designed to modify the weather"—make it rain, that is. Everybody who was seeding the clouds, whether for hire or for experimentation, was required to let the committee know what it was doing.

"If the Advisory Committee finds that weather modification experiments cannot produce important results, it will so report and thus deter farmers and ranchers from spending their money unwisely," Senator Case said, speaking in support of the group's first appropriation.

"If the Advisory Committee finds that weather modification activities work only in certain circumstances, it will find out what these circumstances are and thus encourage feasible projects and discourage those which are not feasible.

"If the Advisory Committee finds out it can confirm the results claimed by the reports it has so far received from reputable and scientifically competent operators—increases of from 7 to 50 percent and more—then the dollar benefits to agriculture, industry, and government will be so great as to be incalculable."

The committee devoted the first six months to doing its homework—studying the subject of rainmaking, meeting with scientists, and going into the field to observe firsthand how seeding was done. It even borrowed some generators and tried some seeding tests on its own. By January 3, 1955, the committee had agreed on the approach it would take to its assignment and, with a competent staff, set to work.

Although it was understood that during the time the President's Advisory Committee on Weather Control was doing its work, the

102

Weather Bureau would refrain from making comments about the subject of cloud-seeding, one way or the other, the word of this restraint seemed not to get around too well among weathermen in the field.

By the spring of 1956, Krick felt obliged to protest directly to Weather Bureau Chief Reichelderfer, sending him a clipping from two newspapers in Florida, the *Lakeland Ledger* and the *Tampa Morning Tribune*, each quoting the local weather bureau man in remarks reflecting a low opinion of cloud-seeding. Since Krick had a seeding project going nearby, these comments were of more than passing interest to him.

"It appears obvious to our client and to our company that these statements . . . are made with the definite intent to minimize any results we might achieve," Krick wrote Reichelderfer. "We shall be pleased to have your comments . . . at your early convenience so that we may determine whether additional action will be required . . ."

Reichelderfer promised, by return mail, to look into the matter. Three weeks later he reported that the instigator appeared to be a reporter who craftily led the weatherman to say things he wouldn't otherwise have said.

"Mr. Johnson [the weatherman in question] reiterated that he is thoroughly familiar with the instructions issued by the Bureau on this subject," the Bureau chief went on. He assured Krick that everything possible was being done "to keep discussions on this controversial subject at the proper scientific level."

In late 1956 Krick was chosen to perform a function for a man he had served before. President Eisenhower's Inaugural Parade Committee selected him to forecast the weather for his second inauguration on January 20 of the new year. Using a Remington Rand Univac computer for the first time, Krick saw that the weather during the period of the inaugural was going to be tricky.

"Our preliminary studies indicate that the major storm of the period may occur at Washington on the night of the twentieth, with conditions beginning to improve on the twenty-first and into the twenty-second," Krick informed C. Langhorne Washburn, chairman of the inaugural committee, near the end of December.

On January 11, with nine days to go, Krick wired Washburn that he was standing by his earlier prediction. "We still expect a stormy period will occur about the twentieth, starting sometime on the nineteenth. Improving conditions are expected on the twenty-first but rather cold and windy . . ."

A week before the ceremony, Krick refined his forecast further. It would be raining up until seven o'clock on the morning of inaugural day, but the cloudiness would break around noon. He advised that Eisenhower be kept indoors until that time. It would then be dry and reasonably clear, with temperatures in the forties. This would be the only break in several days of bad weather.

It all turned out just as Krick predicted. It rained all night, but let up in the morning. The skies cleared, and it was bright and cool for the swearing-in ceremony. Then it resumed raining.

"Right on the head," noted the *Rocky Mountain News*, reminding readers of Krick's forecast that it would be fair and cool. "It was just that—even to having the sun break forth while the President was being sworn in."

Krick's success with the inaugural forecast moved someone at the White House to telephone General Curtis LeMay, chief of the Strategic Air Command, suggesting that LeMay meet with Krick and see if this newest advance in long-range weather forecasting, involving the use of computers, might not have military uses.

General LeMay agreed and Krick twice visited SAC headquarters at Offut Air Force Base, Nebraska, in February and March 1957. "We can make a long-range weather study for strategic targets in adversary countries so that you'll know in advance what kind of weather you'll be up against any time you have to go," he told LeMay.

The general and his staff agreed that it would be a good idea to set up a research program with Krick, to verify what he could do—

to find out how far ahead he could forecast, how close he could come, and how often he could do it.

SAC sent a request for such a program up to Air Force Head-quarters in Washington. There it was channeled to the Air Weather Service, whose chief scientific officer was Dr. Robert D. Fletcher, President of the American Meteorological Society, who recently had warned his colleagues to beware of those who claim the ability to forecast the weather long-range.

The matter was dead.

While Krick was able to stir no more interest at SAC, he did get the attention of the American Meteorological Society. A number of the members had been sending in "newspaper articles and releases regarding claims, attributed to you, on long-range weather forecasting capabilities," Thomas F. Malone, secretary of the AMS, began ominously in a letter to Krick on April 8, 1957.

Malone quoted from a piece in the *Houston Post*, to the effect that "by next spring we will have daily weather charts. We will know what days it will rain in Texas and about how much. We are on the threshold of a dependable method of projecting the weather day by day for several years in advance . . ."

Malone said, "The fact that a number of members of the Society have raised questions requires that our Committee on Professional Ethics and Standards consider the reported claims . . ."

Two "basic questions" were involved, whether Krick had really said the things he was said to have said, and, if so, whether he had ever let the society know what was his basis for saying them—"for their review prior to public announcement."

Krick wrote back that the fundamentals of CalTech's long-range forecasting techniques had first been presented at a national meeting of the AMS at CalTech in June, 1941. Later they were repeated as a special lecture series at the U. S. Weather Bureau in late September and early October, 1941. They were then described in technical papers published by CalTech in 1942 and 1943.

"We have never departed from the basic hypothesis outlined in these discourses and indicated clearly therein, that as data increased we would apply and adapt these techniques to high-speed electronic computers," Krick wrote to Malone.

Krick hopefully interpreted the attention the newspapers were giving to the subject of long-range forecasting as indicating "a healthy and growing interest on the part of the public in the impact of weather upon our lives."

Whatever the public's interest might be, the AMS insisted that long-range forecasting was an impossibility. "Weather forecasts prepared in some detail are possible for two or three days in advance," the society said in a statement issued on July 1, 1957. "The reliability of the prediction, however, decreases progressively after the first day . . ."

The society went on to say that anyone who published forecasts for a month or more in advance, or even for more than two or three days, was misleading the public.

As to where the AMS stood on cloud-seeding, although the President's Advisory Committee on Weather Modification was still gathering information on the topic, the society thought the committee was wasting its time. "Present knowledge of atmospheric processes offers no real basis for the belief that the weather or climate of a large portion of the country can be significantly modified by cloud-seeding," the AMS said in a statement on April 30, 1957, ignoring the fact that Krick had been operating successfully in many countries since 1949.

Weather Bureau Chief Reichelderfer agreed with the AMS. "A review of the extensive experimentation in cloud-seeding which has been undertaken throughout the world, indicates that the results to the present time have been inconclusive and indefinite," he told a House committee holding hearings on a Senate bill to have the National Science Foundation carry on further research after the Eisenhower Committee was finished.

The AMS was soon back with a new lament against Krick. This

time the object of their distress was an article under Krick's name, "Univac Pinpoints the Weather" in the Remington Rand *Systems* Magazine of March-April, 1957. This "may be infringing the Society's code of ethics," AMS Malone wrote Krick, listing the questionable passages in the piece.

To determine whether Krick had indeed overstepped the bounds of the Society's code of ethics, Malone directed him to present himself to the group's Council in New York on Monday, January 27, 1958, at 10:00 A.M., "and be prepared either to refute or substantiate said statements."

Krick replied that the article in question had been written by a writer hired by the Remington Rand Corporation while he was out of the country, but that while he "might have phrased" some of it differently, the piece was essentially correct. Krick wrote that he was going to Europe and therefore would be unable to answer their summons.

Then he mentioned some grievances of his own. Since the Society had gone on record with its statement of July 1, 1957, discarding long-range forecasting as humbug, Krick wrote, it looked to him as if they had already made up their minds and that there was nothing he could say at the meeting to change them.

"It would seem more constructive to have developed a course of action . . . to determine whether we had truly progressed long-range weather forecasting to a point where the broad implications in the Remington Rand *Systems* magazine article were acceptable," he wrote. He chided them for not checking with his group for its opinion before putting out the July 1, 1957, statement that no good forecast could be made beyond three days.

"Tomorrow we shall receive a visitor from one of the major industrial firms in the country," Krick went on. "His instructions from his superiors have been to remain with us as long as is necessary to become completely familiar with our program and its applications to that company's problems. This is the sort of action we had expected General LeMay to receive in answer to his request for a similar evaluation of our work as it affected the operations of the Strategic Air Command ..."

Krick concluded disgustedly, "Our organization and its affiliates have always supported the Society and have continually looked for some signs of the dynamic, forceful leadership which would prove a credit to our science and to our profession. We have not found them."

Krick put the AMS out of his mind, as the President's Committee on Weather Modification, after three years' study, announced its overall findings on December 31, 1957, with a detailed two-volume report to follow in January of the new year. The committee concluded that seeding the clouds with silver iodide from ground generators did, in fact, increase rainfall by 10 to 15 percent in the mountainous states of the West. What the effect was in the flat country of the Plains States, it claimed not to have enough data to tell, although Krick's operations in the Great Plains, covering millions of acres, had been in progress for six years.

The improved rainfall which the committee was able to confirm to its satisfaction was enough to make a substantial difference. A study by Dean A. M. Eberle, of the School of Agriculture at South Dakota State College and vice-chairman of the President's Committee, showed that a mere one percent more rain above normal during the growing season paid the cost of seeding at harvest time.

Seeding from the ground was inexpensive compared to the value of the water it produced, the committee said, not only as it affected agriculture but power companies as well. "Utility organizations in the Pacific Coast area seem to have no doubts as to the value of the precipitation increases they get."

The committee further reported that timely seeding with silver iodide apparently reduced hailstorms by bringing down the rain before the drops had time to freeze into hailstones, or at least into large ones. In this, the committee had in mind the work of Irving Krick, who by this time had experimented with hail control both in the United States and Canada, with seemingly dramatic results.

Information compiled by the Alberta Hail Insurance Board indicated a reduction of 71 percent in wheat losses from hail during the time of Krick's operations to control this scourge. For forty years, on the average, hail had destroyed 13 percent of each year's wheat crop.

The President's Committee enthusiastically saw promise of the day when man might gain a measure of control over the weather, taming its furies as well as increasing the rain. The members strongly advocated a greatly expanded program of research to bring this about.

But to committee chairman Orville, the findings of the group were a disappointment, as revealed by his letter thanking Krick for his help to the committee. "The information you furnished," Orville wrote, "was helpful in arriving at the final conclusions and recommendations (even though they were far too conservative in my opinion.)"

Captain Orville's dissatisfaction with the report stemmed from the successful pressures of the Weather Bureau to water it down. Krick's achievement in the French Alps for Electricité de France, showing increases in snowpack in winter of around 70 percent and annual increases of about 29 percent over historical relationships established between the target and outside control areas, were excluded from the report, as were the results of Krick's work in the Great Plains region, such as his projects to fill reservoirs for Oklahoma City, Dallas and other municipalities.

Although all were reported to the Eisenhower Committee, Krick's massive operations, worldwide, were wholly omitted from the final two-volume publication of the committee's extensive tax-paid survey of the effect of cloud-seeding as a means to increase precipitation.

The scientific establishment, on the other hand, felt that the report of the President's Committee was too sanguine. The scientists suffered "lingering doubts about its reality" and believed that the subject of artificial rainmaking needed a great deal more research.

With nothing settled, there were new hearings on the Senate

measure to have the National Science Foundation take over the quest to learn more. Among the witnesses were Krick and two of his associates, who by this time had operated in twenty-seven states and a dozen foreign countries. Their prepared material included a bibliography of 650,000 hours of seeding time.

Krick testified that he was all for more research but urged that what was already known be put to use. "Where would we be today if we had continued basic research on automobiles . . . say, for twenty years before producing a model car?" he asked rhetorically. "I stress, we need an accelerated well-balanced program, including the actual field operational work. . . .

"Basic research is necessary," he repeated, "but I stress again the importance of the other phases. For instance, during the last fifteen years we have been engaged in a missile race. We have found that all the laboratory and basic research work means little if the missiles won't get off the ground. . . .

"Above all, let us not lose time," Krick urged. "We do not want this important work pushed back into the laboratories for ten years to rehash all that has been done—just for the mere satisfaction of scientists with negative attitudes."

Among others who had something to say at the hearing, including senators, public works officials, ranchers, farmers and bankers, was Merrill J. Langfitt, farm service director for Radio Station KMA, of Shenandoah, Iowa.

"In March of this year," Langfitt said, "Dr. Irving Krick appeared before 700 farmers in the KMA auditorium and told them that his long-range forecast called for above normal precipitation for April, slightly below normal for May, above normal again for June, and slightly below normal for July and August. At the same time he told them they could expect, as a result of cloud-seeding, to have normal or slightly above normal precipitation for the entire growing season.

"Dr. Krick's forecast put new life into our area. Seedsmen started selling seeds, fertilizer sales boomed, bank credit loosened up, retail sales took a spurt, and business in general was very good. Dr. Krick's forecast has held true to this date. I might add that six weeks after Dr. Krick made his forecast, the Weather Bureau came through with essentially the same forecast."

In the end, however, it was decided that before cloud-seeding was admitted to respectable scientific standing, the National Science Foundation should study it some more.

10

The Council Can Delay
No Longer

Though much time had passed, the American Meteorological Society had not forgotten the article under Krick's name in Remington Rand's house organ. On February 24, 1958, nearly three months after Krick had let Secretary Malone know that he would have to miss the January summons to come and discuss the piece, Malone wrote again, repeating the request to meet with them, this time on May 6, in Washington.

"In the event that you do not choose to honor this request," Malone said "the Council can delay no longer and will have to make a finding concerning a possible breach of the Code of Ethics of the Society by you on the basis of the evidence now before it."

Leaving no stone unturned, Malone also wrote to A. C. Hancock, the editor of *Systems*, "to verify statements concerning the authorship of the article, explaining, 'The matter has considerable bearing on a case involving possible breech [sic] of professional ethics by a member of our Society.'"

Did Krick write the piece, Malone asked, or was it written by somebody else hired by the company? If Krick did not write the piece, did he approve it? The company finally confirmed that it, and not Krick, had prepared the offending article.

This in no way dampened the AMS's zeal in getting Krick before them, however. Krick canceled a trip in order to be there on the new date, May 6. As he awaited the appointment with his inquisitors, Krick sought the Society's permission to submit a paper at its National Conference on Practical Problems of Modern Meteorology at Denver in the autumn. "The title of my paper," Krick let them know, "is, Long-Range Forecasting by Electronic Computer," addressing his query to S. B. Beckwith, chairman of the program committee.

Krick included something of what his paper would cover. "If you find the subject of this paper suitable," he wrote, "will you please confirm its acceptance at your early convenience, so that I may plan accordingly."

Chairman Beckwith evidently did not find the subject of long-range weather forecasting suitable to a meeting on the problems of meteorology. "At this time plans are not formed as to the exact program layout," Beckwith replied briefly—and that was that.

As the showdown between Krick and the AMS approached, the Society heard from another quarter in the matter. Krick's longtime mentor, Dr. Theodore von Karman, now chairman of Research and Development at NATO, wrote to them on Krick's behalf with Old World courtesy and somewhat in terms of a Dutch Uncle.

He told how Krick had recognized very early "the economic value of good weather forecasting" and had set up a private consulting service, with Millikan and von Karman's blessings. This was in line with "the free spirit which always prevailed at CalTech for industrial consulting work and other activities of the faculty members. He believed that this "liberal spirit" was responsible for CalTech's success in the field of aeronautics and related industries.

"I also believe," he went on, "that it was shortsighted on the part of the present administration [that of Dr. DuBridge] to cut out Meteorology completely from the curriculum of the Institute."

Then von Karman came to the point: "I do not believe that theoretical solution of the long-range weather forecasting is really established," he wrote. "I am, however, certain that purely theoretical methods cannot be established in the framework of the usual meteorological computations which are essentially two-dimensional. In this situation a half-empirical procedure, as the so-called historical method based on the analysis of a material carefully collected over several decades and analyzed with reasonable mathematical means using recent progresses of the electronic computers, can serve an honest and useful purpose.

"I'm afraid a kind of indictment of such a method on 'ethical' grounds will be considered by the scientific world at present, and especially in the future, as an example of the many narrow-minded professional declarations which have occurred so often in the history of science. I do not think that it is in the interest of the American Meteorological Society to increase the number of such examples."

He proposed that the AMS publish a monograph, written by members of Krick's group, the American Institute of Aerological Research, discussing the development and application of their methods. Then, he suggested, a committee of the Society should be established to confirm and verify the results of their work "within mutually agreed tolerances."

In a nutshell, the AMS should find out what it was talking about before passing judgments.

Krick urged the AMS to follow von Karman's suggestions when he appeared before its council, saying:

"I am convinced that only by this means, or such other as will achieve like results, can the Society perform its full duty to its membership, to the American people, and to the advancement of Science. I shall be delighted to cooperate with any acceptable group you designate and to make my records and staff in Denver, Colorado, available for that purpose."

If the Society refused to make such a study of his work, Krick said he felt that he would be "supporting a policy of static futility, of denial that science is a never ending search for truth," by remaining a member. "In such event," he concluded, "this letter is my resignation from the Society."

Six days after the hearing Secretary Malone informed Krick curtly:

"The Council of the American Meteorological Society has concluded that you have violated the Society's Code of Ethics and finds that it cannot accept the conditions laid down in your statement to the Council dated May 6, 1958."

The refusal of the AMS to inform itself about Krick's long-range forecasting techniques brought a shocked response from Vincent Schaefer, who, along with Irving Langmuir, had discovered how raindrops are made.

"I have read your letter and its enclosures with dismay," Schaefer wrote on June 2, 1958. "The mounting inclination of groups and individuals of varying kinds and disciplines to issue 'pronouncements' on scientific subjects is a disturbing and potentially dangerous activity in the United States. It is in this manner that freedom can be lost. One might be inclined to have a tolerant attitude toward some of this activity if the state of our knowledge were considerably better than it is and those who thought they were being intelligent were more so! If they were, of course, they wouldn't try to do that very thing!"

Max Karant, vice president of the Aircraft Owners and Pilots Association, likewise had some things to say about the AMS action. "We're thoroughly familiar with the rough row being hoed by Dr. Irving P. Krick," he wrote *Business Week*, referring to a piece in the magazine's October 11, 1958, issue: *Charting Weather Years Ahead.*

"We've helped pioneer the use of his techniques in civil aviation, and the results (not theory; results) have at times given us the creeps," Karant went on. "We publish a monthly feature in our

116

magazine called 'AOPA's Weathercast.' Dr. Krick's organization tailors this feature to our specific requirements: specify what weather will be VFR (Visual Flight Rules, with a minimum cloud base of 1000 feet and a minimum of three miles visibility), and what weather will be IFR (Instrument Flight Rules, weather below 1000 feet and three miles). I'm sure you'll admit that this is cutting the weather forecasting business pretty fine."

The feature had been running since March, Karant wrote (and still runs today). At first the group thought of it only as an interesting feature. "But then we began to be brought up short by the general accuracy of the forecasts—prepared for AOPA on an average of three months in advance of the actual publication date. For example, AOPA Weathercast hit that devastating March 19–20 blizzard on the head, while the more conventional weather forecasters were busy beating all around the snowbank within hours of the actual storm. Then, in our September issue, the Weathercast tagged Hurricane Helene within hours of its actual arrival on the East Coast September 27. The forecast was prepared for us in June."

There had been many letters from members amazed by the accuracy of forecasts that far in advance, Karant said, adding that many pilots planned their flights on the Krick feature. "We've also been keeping books on Krick's overall performance—and he's averaging just over 85 percent accurate," he wrote.

"If the eggheads in the meteorology business (with whom we've had many years of experience) regard this sort of record as being the work of a charlatan," Karant commented acidly, "then they'd better start setting up a Charlatan's Division for Scientific Study."

Although Krick was now outside the anointed fold of the American Meteorological Society, the group kept a suspicious eye on him. This was not hard to do, since Krick went on making news.

At the start of 1960, for example, the AMS was vexed to learn that Krick had been named official "weather engineer" for the Winter Olympics to be held at Squaw Valley, California, in

February. It was bad enough to be told that Krick had selected the weather for the games two years earlier, singling out the last two weeks of February as the time best suited to the event. But there was more: Krick would also see to it that there was snow for the occasion, of the right kind and in the right amount.

The northern California chapter of the Society held an emergency meeting and instructed chairman Elmer Robinson to notify the Games' Organizing Committee of the Society's "concern and displeasure" with Krick's appointment. Accordingly, Chairman Robinson duly warned the Organizing Committee how important it was that "as a public body (it) not fall into a promotional trap."

Robinson added, "In addition, our group is not happy with the fact that the man selected by the Organizing Committee is not an AMS member and therefore not bound by the Society's concept of professional ethics." For instance, Robinson pointed out, Krick had picked the weather for the games two years before. "In the opinion of the Society," he said, "this is a scientific impossibility. To call these 'forecasts' does meteorology a disservice."

Krick planted twenty generators about the valley. Since there was little or no snow in sight for November or December, he first fired up the generators in November, starting quintillions of silver iodide particles drifting into the winter sky. He waited, then fired up again on January 8, 9, and 10.

On the morning of January 10 seven feet of snow covered the ski slopes and three-and-a-half feet mantled the valley floor. The perennial bugbear of insufficient snow for the winter Olympics seemed "pretty well dispelled a month before the opening of the VIII Olympic Winter Games," wrote Gladwin Hill of the New York *Times* on January 24.

"A heavy mantle of snow, forty to eighty inches deep, blankets the floor and slope of this Sierra Nevada mountain basin, where 800 athletes from some thirty nations soon will be converging," Hill wrote.

To give people a chance to get there, Krick let up on the seeding a few days before the events were to start. On the final night, he fired up the generators a final time, "to provide a good snow base and quality for the Games."

As a crowning touch, just as the ceremonies opened, the clouds broke apart and the sun came through, brightly bathing the scene in sunlight while the Olympic flame was lighted. This was too much for the Russians. Eagerly they crowded around the interpreters and asked, "Have the Americans perfected weather control?"

When the games were over, Krick received a grateful note from H. D. Thoreau, managing director for the Organizing Committee of the Games, saying, "We were, indeed, fortunate in the selection of our dates for the Games from the standpoint of good weather."

The American Meteorological Society, however, remained inflexibly unimpressed. At the National Farm Directors' meeting in Chicago in November, 1960, the AMS was on hand to see that no one got slickered into the notion that better weather forecasting was just around the corner. The society passed out copies of its July 1, 1957, statement that forecasts of two or three days ahead are about the best any honest man can do, and anybody who says he can go out a month or more is misleading the public.

It wasn't long after this that Krick had a golden new opportunity to demonstrate once again what the AMS doggedly insisted had never been demonstrated. "In going over reports of the Inauguration of four years ago," wrote Tyler Abell, vice-chairman of the Inaugural Committee, to Krick on December 13, 1960, "I noted you accurately predicted fair weather while everyone else was sorrowfully saying the Eisenhower luck had run out. . . . I understand that you are very much of an Eisenhower man, and predicted the weather for the President for years, but hope that you will help out the Inaugural Committee again, even though a Democrat is being sworn in this time."

Krick provided the forecast for the inauguration of John F. Kennedy on January 20 by return mail—so promptly that he felt obliged to explain. Since the Eisenhower inaugural in 1957, he wrote, they had greatly expanded their UNIVAC computer facilities, now located in Zurich, Switzerland.

"At this location we are performing the task of extending the evolution of weather events throughout the world for many years into the future," Krick wrote. "I give you this information lest you gain the impression that my immediate reply to your letter implies a lack of thorough study and investigation before issuing the Inaugural Forecast. Actually, the information from which it was derived was transmitted to Denver from our laboratories in Zurich in 1959 and is the basis for many studies and reports issued to our clients for the year 1961."

Krick's forecast for Washington on Inauguration Day, nearly six weeks away, called for "fair weather, with no precipitation. However, it will be cold," Krick predicted. "Snow may accompany a storm a few days prior to January 20 but there should be time to clear the streets following it. Another period of stormy weather will arrive in Washington late January 21 or 22. Therefore January 20 will simply be one of the days of fair weather between storms.

"In predicting weather events of this kind, pinpointed to a specific city," Krick wrote, "we maintain an accuracy in our timing of less than one day. Therefore I feel that you can go forward with complete assurance that the weather will not upset your plans."

As all who watched the inauguration of President Kennedy on January 20, 1961, will recall, the day was clear, with the sun shining brightly on the newly fallen snow—and it was cold: twenty-two degrees, just as Krick had said it would be a month and a half before.

Krick made his inaugural prediction at about the time the American Meteorological Society, in its December bulletin, published an editorial which again raised the hackles of Max Karant of the Aircraft Owners and Pilots Association. Karant took it as a personal affront and protested in an irate letter to AMS secretary Malone.

"One of our members has just sent us a photostat of your editorial 'Society Policy on Ethics' in the December bulletin," Karant began. "He particularly marked the paragraph in which you refer to 'quackery'. . . . You refer to 'wildly extravagant claims' and 'a spectacular story in the press or trade magazine. . . .'

"This is of particular interest to me because (1) we happen to have one of the larger trade magazines, (2) we publish such material, which makes us eligible for the 'quackery' charge, and (3) our particular group of people (87,000 pilots and plane owners) probably have had more continuous, detailed, and often-frightening dealings with the ethical meteorologists I gather you represent than has any other comparable group.

"In the first place the term 'quackery' is synonymous with 'fake' and 'untrue,'" Karant continued hotly. "Our experience with the long-range forecast material we buy from the Krick organization . . . has been surprisingly good, on the factual record. Is this still 'quackery'?

"And, speaking for myself only, I would say that, in attempting to use airplanes for transportation, I have had my life literally placed in jeopardy by presumably 'pure' professional meteorologists so many times over so many years that it might even warrant a little closer attention to this 'quackery' of which you speak. As a pilot whose safety is constantly affected by the accuracy and reliability of the meteorologist, I'm a good deal more interested in better forecasting—by whatever system—than I am in the traditional preoccupation of the scientist with his sacrosanct scientific journal."

President Kennedy had not been long in office when, perhaps influenced by Krick's inaugural forecast, he indicated an interest in improved weather prediction and control. His remarks prompted Krick to wire the President advising him of a forthcoming discussion on these subjects between himself and Dave Garroway on Garroway's NBC "Today" television show. "During the past decade," Krick charged, "the U.S. has allowed the initiative in applying known techniques in precise long-range weather forecasting and control as developed in this country to pass to other NATO nations."

Krick's message to Kennedy was referred to Weather Bureau Chief Reichelderfer, who replied with one of his forward defenses of the service. Then he wrote a personal "Dear Irv" letter to Krick, sounding more plaintive than angry:

"Dear Irv: You and I have known each other for more than twenty years. I have always been open to frank and direct suggestions. If you felt as you indicated in your telegram to the President, why didn't you say something about it when we saw each other in New York in January? After all of these years of advancement of the science how do we interpret a move like your telegram?"

Krick replied with twelve single-spaced pages, unloading a long accumulation of grievances. "You and I both know that 'official meteorology' in the U.S. has little competence in either precise long-range forecasting or weather control," he wrote, commenting that he found Reichelderfer's letter "typical of all correspondence between us in the past twenty years."

He accused the Weather Bureau of shrugging off any advances coming from outside its own circle. "Precise long-range weather forecasting . . . requires day-by-day prediction for years ahead." This had to come first—before there could be any large-scale planning of weather control operations. "To my knowledge our group is the only one in the world today successfully applying these principles. Now that other nations are using our results effectively, why isn't the United States?"

Krick accused the American Meteorological Society of continuing to reject the evidence of advancement in long-range weather forecasting, dismissing such forecasting as quackery. He accused the AMS of "steadfastly maintaining a closed mind," and of glossing over the need to look at new knowledge.

He cited the refusal of the AMS to consider the proposal of Theodore von Karman—"a world leader in science and technology and a man known by the AMS to be intimately familiar with our work"—that the Society look into Krick's methods. "Their refusal to examine the evidence supporting our claims (was) unworthy of a professional society representing itself to the public as a scientific body."

Forecasting by the United States Weather Bureau had not improved, Krick charged, despite the help of "globe-circling weather surveillance satellites, electronic computers and all of the modern paraphernalia with which to rapidly process weather information." What it lacked, he said, was "a valid method of forecasting." Without this, programmed to the machines, all the Bureau could hope for was to go on turning out "imperfect predictions with increasing rapidity, permitting the Weather Bureau to disseminate them to a greater segment of the population resulting in a continuing decline in the 'weatherman's' public image."

Krick reviewed the record of success which his CalTech system had met with in World War II and in the years since, enabling him and his associates to set up a worldwide weather forecasting and control service.

"If you and others had been completely unaware of Rossby's [Professor Carl] attempts to vitiate our work over a period of many years," Krick went on, "there might be some excuse for the present attitude of the Weather Bureau and the view of the AMS. However, the dangers of Rossby's program to discredit the CalTech meteorologists and the impact it might have on the evolution of this science in the U. S. for many years to come, were outlined to you fully in a letter from Dr. Robert A. Millikan dated July 3, 1943. . . .

"Will the United States be forever penalized because official meteorology in this country can neither comprehend basic scientific truths nor evaluate evidence of their successful application?"

What heritage had Professor Rossby left to the United States? "His followers are unable to progress weather forecasting because Rossby's basic premises, on which they work, are invalid. . . . Since his decease, the Weather Bureau still clings to these methods. Thus the United States literally and figuratively has placed its weather forecasting bets on a dead horse."

11

You Have Not
Published Your Data

Krick sent a copy of his Reichelderfer letter to President Kennedy, since it pretty well traced the history of what had been going on in United States weather forecasting circles for the past twenty-five years or so. He was not encouraged by the reply that change was imminent.

The answer came from Professor Jerome Wiesner, Special Assistant to the President for Science and Technology, who had come to his White House post from MIT. Wiesner wrote coolly that he had not been able to find a good scientific explanation of Krich's position in the technical journals. Krick, in reply, offered Wiesner his organization's thirty years of scientific, academic and engineering experience. He did not hear from Wiesner again.

With the space age beginning and Colonel John Glenn set to orbit the earth, the ability to forecast the weather some time in advance was important to the National Aeronautics and Space Administration, especially since weather was involved both at the launch site and the recovery area.

Through the office of Senator Robert Kerr, Chairman of the Aeronautical and Space Sciences Committee, Krick arranged a meeting with Dr. Abe Silverstein, Director of Space Flight for NASA. Afterward, following his custom, Krick summarized their discussion in a letter to Silverstein, with a copy to James Webb, NASA's chief.

Two courses of action were open, Krick suggested—waiting until the meteorological establishment woke up to what can be done, or going ahead with what was already working.

"Since our whole system functions within the framework of ultra long-range weather forecasts of useful accuracy," Krick wrote, "a practical test of the potential of such an approach could be provided by utilizing long-range forecasts for planning NASA space flights. Such a program would avoid the uncertainties of weather resulting in delays or cancellations of scheduled flights. By establishing specifications for each flight operation, periods free of weather complications could be chosen in advance."

NASA's number two man, Deputy Administrator Hugh L. Dryden, replied that the U.S. Weather Bureau was supplying NASA with both long- and short-range forecasts for their space shots.

Krick tried again. Mailing off an offer of his forecasting services to Dryden, Krick sent a copy to his old friend, von Karman, asking him to give a hand in persuading NASA officials that he could help sharpen their weather forecasts. If they didn't like his work, Krick pointed out, "they could always fire us! Certainly, they could not be criticized for trying, in view of weather difficulties that seem apparent at present."

The weather difficulties Krick referred to had already caused the cancellation of Colonel Glenn's flight on January 27, 1962, from Cape Canaveral. It need not have been, Krick wrote to his representative in Congress, Peter Dominick, who had asked for Krick's views on the forecasts provided NASA by the Weather Bureau.

"We were asked by WISN-TV in Milwaukee, one of our clients, to make a forecast last Friday for the flight Saturday," Krick explained, enclosing a copy of the script. He had predicted cloudiness for the morning of the shot, "but did not expect this to last long enough to require cancellation of the flight."

The weather did, in fact, clear around ten o'clock, contrary to the expectations of government forecasters at the launch site, but by that time the flight had already been scrubbed.

The Glenn flight was rescheduled for Thursday, February 1. On Tuesday, January 30, Mutual's KOSI in Denver asked Krick for his ideas on the weather for the new date. He predicted that conditions would be unfavorable at both ends: at the launch site, a heavy ground fog; in the recovery area, heavy swells and cloudiness.

A few hours after Krick's broadcast, NASA again cancelled the launching without explanation.

There were more new dates for the launching, and more cancellations. The space agency was still waiting for the right kind of weather to turn up when Dryden gave Krick a curt brushoff on his letter repeating the offer of his services. Krick kept his temper and tried again. The answer was still no.

Dryden sent the same word to von Karman, who had indeed taken a hand on Krick's behalf. It was "not practical to substitute Dr. Krick for the U. S. Weather Bureau in the operational forecasts for Project Mercury," he wrote.

Colonel Glenn was still on the ground when Krick wrote to Congressman Dominick that the time had come "to get this matter out in the open. I believe that the Weather Bureau and segments of our profession who continue to disclaim that long-range forecasting is possible and push for hundreds of millions of dollars in research money to find a method of doing the job, are not only dishonest, but do a distinct disservice to our country by deterring agencies like NASA from seeking help outside the government when it is sorely needed. Certainly somebody is going to start asking questions before long to find out why NASA can't get a forecast for twenty-four hours."

Colonel Glenn finally got off on his three orbits of the earth on February 20, 1962, more than three weeks later.

12

Our Name Has No Bearing on the Subject

In early August, 1962, Krick at last received an opportunity to show the space industry something of what he could do. He was invited to address a joint meeting of the Institute of Aerospace Sciences and the American Rocket Society on August 31.

"As I understand it," Krick wrote to Ernest L. Kistler of the Martin Marietta Corporation, Denver Division, who had issued the invitation and would be chairman of the meeting, "the interest is in the methods of ultra-long long-range forecasting which have been developed by our organization. Therefore I suggest as a title for my talk, 'Year-Ahead Predictions of Atmospheric Conditions as an Aid in Planning Space Shots.' "

To add interest to the occasion, Krick suggested that the program include a simulated briefing for a manned space shot. "Engineers in your company will have approximate dates for such shots in the future," Krick wrote. If he could have some of these dates a little ahead of time, he indicated, he would pick the one best suited to the shot from a weather standpoint.

Kistler agreed and within the week the Martin company provided

Krick with a theoretical spaceshot problem. They asked Krick's permission to make copies of the problem and distribute them at the meeting. "This should impress them with the complexity of your forecast work," wrote Jerold M. Bidwell, of the company's Meteorological Support Group, who likewise asked for a copy of Krick's forecast when it was ready, "as an example of the type of work your company can do for a complicated missile launch."

The imaginary space shot problem formulated by Martin's engineers was "to schedule a manned rendezvous-type mission so that no delay will be experienced due to weather. At H-hour a missile carrying a logistics payload will be launched into an orbit from Cape Canaveral, Florida." This would be followed after a specified interval by a manned shot to rendezvous with the first. This second shot must be fired "during daylight hours" and with a delay of no more than one minute. "The mission should be scheduled during the calendar month of February, 1963."

All details were spelled out, as if it were to be a real launching. "About 12 hours would be needed to prepare the logistics shot for launching," the problem went on. "If the wind speed including gusts at 100 feet is expected to exceed 50 knots at the launch site during the 12-hour period, the launch will be delayed." There was need to know how hard the wind was blowing beyond 25 knots at the surface, plus or minus 5 knots, and for how long during the 12 hours before launch.

"Launch will not be carried out if wind speeds greater than 175 knots are anticipated between 25,000 and 50,000 feet altitude," the statement continued. "The vehicle will not be launched during a thunderstorm or so that the vehicle will pass through a thunderhead. The vehicle must not pass through rain or hail, but can take drizzle. . . . It is required that the entire missile be visible at the blockhouse at launch—distance 1500 feet.

"It is required that the missile be visually tracked to 100,000 feet. This requires no haze aloft, 25 miles visibility, and less than one-tenth cloud coverage at the Cape Canaveral launch site.

The specifications continued, "In the event of abort, the impact area of the payload should have greater than 10 miles visibility, no haze aloft below 10,000 feet, and less than one-tenth cloud coverage below 10,000 feet. Clouds above 10,000 feet must not interfere with radar. Surface wind must neither exceed a mean value of 20 knots nor have gusts greater than 25 knots. Wave heights must be less than 5 feet. . . . This requirement will hold from Cape Canaveral to ascension."

The statement ended: "Problem prepared by the Martin Meteorological Support Group."

Krick was delighted with the challenge. It was like Normandy all over again. He wrote a memorandum to Paul E. Ruch, one of his vice presidents, attaching a copy of the Martin problem. "We are to develop this forecast for presentation at my IAS-ARS talk at the Martin Company on August 31," Krick explained.

"I should like a staff study, setting up requirements for this forecast by August 24. We will require such things as: should there be an absence of the jet stream; should we do the shots just after a cold-front passage in the high-pressure area behind it, and so on. . . .

"After we have decided what we are looking for," Krick instructed Ruch, "then several of us should go through the progs (prognostic weather charts) for February, 1963, and the analogs, to determine which time we should select. One of the problems, of course, will be the possible abort between Canaveral and ascension. We will have to look at the European maps in conjunction with the North American maps. . . .

"If we can get our shots off on a one-two basis, it will save refueling, the costs of clearing the range for such a long period, and other factors of substantial economic importance."

Krick optimistically saw it all as a golden chance to get the door open to them at Martin to work with the company on some real space launchings in the future.

At the August 31 meeting, held in the Martin company cafeterias, Krick first told something of his background. Then he re-stated the problem submitted by Martin calling for a time in February, 1963, some six months away, best suited to firing a couple of men into space and having them join up with a logistics shot sent up the day before.

Krick gave as the best interval for the mission February 6 to 10.

Dr. George Reynolds, member of the American Meteorological Society and one of the three comprising Martin's Meteorological Support Group who had worked up the problem for Krick, dis-agreed with Krick's forecast. Reynolds said it was highly unlikely that five consecutive days of the kind of weather needed would occur at any time at all in February.

Krick politely countered that he and three of his associates had each considered the problem independently and that all four men had come to the same finding as to the five-day period selected. Krick recommended that the logistics shot be sent up on February 6, followed by the manned shot next morning at eleven o'clock, Eastern Standard Time.

In the informal discussion which developed after the meeting, Martin engineers remarked that they hoped the dates Krick had given, February 6 and 7, 1963, might be used for an actual shot of special importance to the Martin company. Krick would have reason to recall the comment in due course.

A few days after the August 31 meeting Krick documented his forecast in a letter to Jerold Bidwell: "Although the problem was fictitious, the forecast was an actual prediction which you may wish to verify in February of 1963. . . . I am sure we shall all be watching the weather next February to see how it turns out."

Krick evidently had been a hit with his audience. Chairman Ernest Kistler wrote him on September 5, thanking him for an excellent presentation.

Krick had done so well, in fact, that he was booked to repeat his talk at the IAS Aerospace Reliability and Maintainability Con-ference to be held in Washington, D.C., May 6 to 8. By that time the forecast he had made for Martin's hypothetical space launchings in February would have been verified, as he confidently wrote to Frank A. Thompson, chief of Martin's Systems Reliability section. He said he would expand his new talk to include an explanation of how he and his associates arrived at the prediction.

As February, 1963, approached, Krick waited to see how close he came with his forecast for the "insoluble" problem provided by the Martin firm back in August. On the morning of February 6, the day he had selected for the first shot, a headline leaped at him from the front page of the *Denver Post*: 6,500 MILES—TITAN II LIFTS TOP PAYLOAD.

Under a Cape Canaveral dateline, the story led off, "A *Titan II* intercontinental ballistic missile carried the heaviest military payload in United States history for a record distance of 6,500 miles Wednesday in a test flight from Cape Canaveral, Florida . . ."

Krick remembered the remarks of Martin engineers after the August meeting that they hoped the February dates might be used for a space launch of particular significance to the Martin company. He remembered the remarks all over again next day when yet a new headline from Cape Canaveral proclaimed: POLARIS MAKES 1,800-MILE TRIP DOWN ATLANTIC.

There could hardly be more flattering verification of Krick's Martin forecast than these headlines. Mention of the *Titan* and *Polaris* shots worked in nicely with an updating of his August paper, "Precise Year-Ahead Predictions of Atmospheric Conditions for Aerospace Operations," which he planned to deliver at the aerospace meeting in Washington on May 6.

The flights of the *Titan* and *Polaris* dramatically demonstrated what Krick had long been shouting to the wind—that he and his group were able to make detailed and accurate forecasts far into the future for a given day and place.

Krick's elation lasted until he got back the advance copy of his paper for the May meeting which he had submitted to Reynolds and Bidwell for their comments. Writing on plain paper—no more

Martin company letterheads—these two members of the American Meteorological Society purported to remain unconvinced of Krick's long-range forecasting ability.

It would be fine if it could be done, they agreed, but "the real question has been the accuracy of such forecasts," they wrote, adding "obviously we have tried to keep an open mind on the problem."

The pair had another objection to Krick's paper. They complained that the several references to the Martin company was likely to mislead the readers and listeners into thinking that the Martin company was endorsing Krick's operations.

"The cooperation you have received was by individuals, as individuals, in cooperation with IAS professional activity," they wrote. "It is coincidental that they were employed by the Martin Company."

Reynolds and Bidwell came at length to the matter of the two missile shots which Martin had fired on February 6 and 7, the dates Krick had selected for hypothetical launchings nearly six months earlier.

"The flights of the *Titan II* and *Polaris* are really irrelevant," they wrote. "The design criteria for these vehicles and missions are undoubtedly quite different than those set forth in the problem statement." They objected to mention of the two launchings in Krick's paper for the May 6 meeting because it was "likely to confuse the listener," causing him to think that since the missions were successful, Krick's forecast was obviously correct.

The two-page critique of Krick's paper ended with the dictum that there be no reference to the Martin Company, to Dr. George Reynolds, or to Mr. Jerold M. Bidwell.

Krick was still mulling the Reynolds-Bidwell document when, in a few days, he received an alarmed letter from W. D. McBride, the Martin company's public relations director, who wrote that he had just seen a copy of Krick's paper, "Precise Year-Ahead Predictions of Atmospheric Conditions for Aerospace Operations." McBride demanded that Krick remove "all references to the Martin Company in both the oral and printed presentation of this subject paper."

The fact that the August meeting had been held on Martin company premises and that Martin engineers had worked up the space shot problem, or that a Martin man had reviewed Krick's paper— none of this had anything to do with the Martin company, McBride insisted. Everyone had been acting on behalf of the Institute of Aerospace Sciences. Therefore, "the use of our name has no bearing on the subject."

McBride ended by saying, "I presume you appreciate our position in this matter and will take the necessary steps to make the changes to your presentation."

In his surprise, Krick assumed McBride had not been fully informed about the Martin firm's role in the evolvement of the paper in question and ran through the story for him.

"Thus," he wrote, "the Martin Company has, in fact, played a useful part in not only assisting in the resolution of a scientific controversy, but opening up a new operational capability in the Aerospace Industry. After all, it was not the IAS that fired the *Titan II* at Cape Canaveral on February 6, 1963, on the basis of the IAS-ARS meeting August 31, 1962!"

Krick concluded, "Frankly, after the *Titan II* shot on February 6, 1963, we expected the Martin Company to approach us for the purpose of issuing a joint statement on the basis [of Chairman Kistler's promise to give credit where credit is due]. Possibly this was the first shot ever planned months in advance for a specific date and time and then so fired."

Krick sent his paper to the May 6 meeting, but under the circumstances felt it pointless to attend. Instead, he flew to Europe to visit his old and ailing friend, von Karman, who, alas, died while Krick was still over the Atlantic.

Krick was missed at the meeting more than he had reason to expect. "The Program Committee . . . was greatly distressed that you did not appear to present your paper," wrote John de S. Coutinho of the Grumman Aircraft Engineering Company, adding that about 100 people had asked for copies of Krick's paper.

This news encouraged Krick to hope that he might get the paper published in the journal of the AIAA. Again, no—because the paper had never been presented at one of the organization's meetings.

So Krick was neither heard nor read on the proposition that accurately forecasting the weather far in advance for the space industry was now a demonstrated truth.

13

We Are Not Lacking
in Research

Faring better in getting his views published was Dr. Walter Orr Roberts, Director of the National Center for Atmospheric Research near Boulder, Colorado. The day was not far off when man would know how to make reliable long-range weather forecasts, hopefully declared Dr. Roberts in *Western Water News* for July and August, 1965.

Established in 1960, NCAR's mission was to "provide a focal point for a vigorous national effort in the atmospheric sciences that draw together scientists from many disciplines and provide the necessary support and facilities for research on important problems of the atmosphere," one of its leaflets explained. The enterprise was supported by the National Science Foundation and operated by the nonprofit University Corporation for Atmospheric Research, comprising more than forty universities from Massachusetts to California.

"One major goal of atmospheric research has always been to improve our ability to predict the weather accurately," the leaflet continued. "Aided by new technological developments such as radar and weather satellites, the weather forecasters have improved their accuracy a great deal over the past few decades. However, it still is not possible to make very precise forecasts of weather more than a couple of days in advance," the tract said, leaving the reader to wonder in what way forecasting had improved.

NCAR was one of many such government undertakings which began proliferating after Langmuir and Schaefer discovered the secret of rainmaking, starting with the military's Project Cirrus in 1947 to check out with further experiments what Langmuir and Schaefer had discovered.

As ever more government agencies got into the experimental cloud-seeding act, all more or less duplicating one another's work, it became virtually ritualistic in each new congress to call for legislation to put somebody in overall charge of the government's researches in weather modification.

Finally, in 1961, Congress tagged the Bureau of Reclamation to be the ball carrier in these studies. Out of this came "Project Skywater . . . to explore, develop, and eventually apply the technology of weather modification to meet the Nation's increasing demand for clean water."

There would be lots of money for lots of people for a long time. The job was "recognized in the mid-1960s as at least an $800 million task over a period of twenty years."

By law the Bureau of Reclamation classified all its seeding operations in the field as "experimental." This hobbled the work of private operators such as Krick by keeping them at least 150 miles from any area where the government was at work.

In 1966, its "lingering doubts" put to rest by ten more years of research, the National Academy of Sciences cautiously reaffirmed what the Eisenhower Committee on Weather Modification had announced in 1957—that cloud-seeding does indeed help it to rain. It was now time to try to get the government to add some operational cloud-seeding to its experiments—that is, seeding to bring rain as well as information.

138

Two bills were introduced in the Senate, S.23 and S.2916. The first directed the Secretary of the Interior, working with the National Science Foundation, to seed for rain in at least five regions of the United States. There would be $20 million for this. The second bill called for an eight-year program of research under the Secretary of Commerce into all aspects of weather control—fog, hail, hurricanes, tornadoes. For this project there would be no limit on the money, but "such sums as may be necessary."

"It is apparent that 1966 should be a year of action," hopefully observed Peter Dominick, now a Colorado Senator, as he opened hearings on the two bills before the Committee on Commerce in Denver on March 31.

Once again, as at the hearings ten years earlier, to have the National Science Foundation go on with the research, Krick and his men were on hand to testify. What they had to contribute took up sixty pages of the official transcript of the proceedings. Since Langmuir and Schaefer made their historic discovery in 1946, Krick testified, he and his organization had conducted more than two million generator hours of operation in twenty-nine states, seven provinces of Canada, Mexico, Central America, the West Indies, Spain, France, the Alps, Italy, Sardinia, Israel, Syria, North Africa and the Congo.

"Some projects have been operated consecutively for fourteen years," Krick said. Clients included a United States government agency, foreign governments, state and provincial governments, counties, towns, chemical corporations, paper and pulp companies, power and utility firms, ski tows, farmers, ranchers, and others. "In our testimony," Krick said, "we have listed something over 100 of these projects with a bibliography of the reports which have been made in an attempt to evaluate results."

In the overall they had increased precipitation by 15 to 30 percent. In the United States they had reduced hail damage to crops by 70 to 80 percent, and in Canada from 60 to 90 percent.

"Since 1951 we have advocated that significantly important

benefits could accrue within the major watershed areas of the West by augmenting natural precipitation through weather modification. The knowledge and engineering are available. . . . We are not lacking in research. . . . We have provided all of our own data to the National Science Foundation at no charge."

Krick pointed out that what he and his organization were saying now was about the same as ten years before. "At that time we urged the findings of President Eisenhower's Advisory Committee be recognized as a valid accomplishment, that man had indeed increased precipitation by 9 to 17 percent based on studies of commercial cloud-seeding projects. We urged that this knowledge be utilized without further loss of time."

Krick charged that between the findings of the Eisenhower Committee and the current report of the National Academy of Sciences upholding them, ten years had been lost. "Now, again, unless positive action is taken, another ten years could be lost debating the relative merits of such programs," he warned, with more prophecy than he knew. "We see no reason for any further delay in activating operational programs here to augment national precipitation."

Krick said weather modification was the cheapest way to get more water and food. "Present knowledge must be applied broadly and without delays," he urged. "The fruits of further research may be incorporated as they become valid."

Senator Dominick's cheerful prediction that 1966 "should be a year of action" proved to be a poor one. The Senate passed S.2916, but too late in the session for the House to act; bills to modify the weather went on being a routine exercise of each new congress.

Two years later, in 1968, Senator Dominick introduced a bill of his own, S.2058, with the specific purpose of bringing more rain and snow to the upper Colorado River region in order to increase the stream flow of this vital watercourse. His bill called for seeding operations to be carried on by experienced private companies that had proved what they could do. At the same time, to mollify the diehard skeptics, there would be money to evaluate their work by independent groups as it proceded.

Again, nothing happened; the bill died. "If this program as envisioned by Dominick in 1968 had gone through," Krick said flatly in the summer of 1977, "the present grim water prospects along the Colorado would not be present—there would be enough water for everybody."

In the fall of 1969, Krick forecast that the country would be hit by severe droughts during the decade of the 1970s. "Quite likely the early part of the decade will not be the critical period, but drought conditions could be as dominant by 1975 as they were in the fifties and thirties," Krick wrote in the October issue of *The Farmer-Stockman*, published in Oklahoma City and widely read by farmers and ranchers of the Southwest.

"Our basic long-range forecasting technique has been permitting us to construct pressure charts into the seventies already, and persistent dryness is not indicated to be firmly set until then," Krick wrote. "Western halves of Kansas, Oklahoma and Panhandle-Texas will be most exposed to droughts."

By the spring of 1971, just as Krick had forecast, the Oklahoma plains lay scorching under a burning sun as high-riding clouds drifted mockingly by, leaving no rain behind. Winds threatened soon to carry away the topsoil, restoring the dread dust-bowl days of the "Dirty Thirties." At stake was Oklahoma's billion-dollar farm and ranch economy, with all the melancholy implications which this held for the rest of the nation. Much of the wheat crop was already lost.

"The present drouthy conditions confirm Dr. Krick's expressions on the subject given in the October 1969 *The Farmer-Stockman*," wrote Ferdie Deering, editor and publisher of the periodical, in the April issue. He reminded his readers that the worst "drouth years of the seventies are still ahead."

Deering compared Krick's forecast to the one he made in 1946 predicting the severe drought of the 1950s. He told how Krick's organization at that time had "mounted a gigantic cloud-seeding effort which relieved millions of acres of farm and ranch land as well as water supply for such cities as Lawton, Oklahoma City, Dallas, Fort Worth, and many others."

The same measures could now help again if they were started soon enough, Deering wrote. He pointed out that "some of the early farm and ranch projects have been operated continuously since the fifties and have been pretty well immunized against drouth."

As July came and the new drought worsened, Deering directed increasing attention to Krick, whose long-range forecasts his publication had carried as a regular feature for twenty-five years, because the best they had been able to get from the Weather Bureau "was a report on what the weather had been in the same month a year earlier." That, Deering wrote, wasn't "a whole lot of help."

Deering recalled that Krick, as he made his long-range forecasts, began advancing the idea of seeding the clouds for more moisture, stirring up "a considerable amount of controversy, largely generated by government bureaucrats. They weren't providing long-range forecasts and they didn't believe in cloud-seeding, but they didn't want anybody else fooling around with the weather, which they seemed to regard as their own 'private public property.' "

By August 1971, when it was so dry that, as one rancher joked, "Out our way we'd need two inches of rain just to make it run off the blacktop road," Ferdie Deering reminded his readers that it had been nearly two years since *The Farmer-Stockman* published Krick's forecast of the current drought. It had now asked Krick how long he thought the drought would last and presented his answer:

"In our opinion this drought started in 1970 and will continue to spread, probably peaking out around 1975. Characteristic signs are readily apparent in areas such as western Oklahoma, west Texas, and southern New Mexico. We anticipate the drouth, as it develops, will spread northward and eastward, working on up into states as far north as Illinois."

That reply, Deering wrote, made him think it was time to do

something about the weather, but he had little hope that anything would be done.

"The basic potential of cloud-seeding to increase rainfall has been well known for more than a quarter of a century," he pointed out. "The U. S. Weather Bureau, now the National Weather Service, has resisted, denied, and ridiculed the entire idea for years, and is widely regarded as being largely responsible for delaying application of weather modification."

Meanwhile, a fourteen-man "weather modification study committee," named by Oklahoma's Governor Hall with Ferdie Deering as chairman, recommended to the governor that a cloud-seeding plan submitted by Krick be accepted. Krick proposed to install forty silver iodide generators 100 miles or so into Texas, each pouring forth 500 thousand billion silver iodide crystals a minute into the rising currents as likely looking clouds approached.

Krick guaranteed to bring down 20 to 30 percent more rain than otherwise could be expected in the target area of 10,000 square miles of the state's total of 70,000 square miles. Krick's rainmaking program would go on for a year, and his price was slightly over two cents an acre—$162,000 altogether.

Two days later the U.S. Bureau of Reclamation came in with a cloud-seeding scheme of its own—not to last a year but one month. The cost would be $210,000. The Bureau's plan was, of course, "experimental," meaning that the emphasis, as customary, was on research rather than applying proven techniques—and that private operators like Krick would have to keep any seeding projects of their own at least 150 miles away in order not to "contaminate" the government's experiments.

The Bureau of Reclamation planned to assault the clouds with ammonium nitrate, a fertilizer and explosive, spewing it from a giant C-97 cargo plane fitted with nozzles, after a pair of light planes with radar and flying ahead like coon dogs on a scent, picked out the clouds to hit.

There would also be a plane to fly through the rain to measure it. This touch of razzle-dazzle was too much for one member of Governor Hall's committee. "We will measure the rain if somebody will produce it," he snapped.

The vote of the governor's committee went to Krick, but the Bureau of Reclamation had money—Oklahoma didn't. So Krick was shoved aside. For Senator Dominick it finally was one too many experiments by the government at a time when the need for rain was critical, and he let fly with a straight-talking speech on the floor of the Senate on August 5, 1961.

"Weather modification is the unfortunate victim of a pervasive bureaucratic attitude—in segments of both the government and academia—that it must remain in the category of a research project, perhaps ad infinitum," Dominick began. "After a quarter of a century of permitting a special segment of the scientific community to sit on cloud-seeding as if it were some kind of illegitimate egg, we are—I repeat, after a quarter century—at a point where we should be able to use it as a prime weapon to fight drought. Instead, we find ourselves being told the egg isn't ready to hatch. . . .

"After the Wright Brothers proved that it was possible to fly a heavier-than-air craft," Dominick went on, "the research that followed and continues today was not to prove that one could fly, but rather to improve on the means and method of flight. In my opinion, far too much of the governmental activity associated with cloud-seeding has been directed toward repeating what Doctors Schaefer, Langmuir, and Vonnegut—the Wright Brothers of cloud-seeding—proved in 1946."

The senator referred to the ten years it had taken the National Science Foundation to confirm, in 1966, what the Eisenhower Committee on Weather Modification had found out in 1957. "Now here we are five years later," he reminded his colleagues, and the research was going on more furiously than ever. The Bureau of Reclamation had thirteen cloud-seeding projects going, "all listed in the realm of research" and involving at least eight major government agencies.

Dominick called for a "standardized plan of operation, which could be set in motion to apply to any drought-affected area of the country. When drought strikes," he concluded, "we should be able to call on cloud-seeding experts immediately, not after a drought has taken a firm hold, and for the future, we must be able to predict these droughts and prevent them by advance operations."

To no one's surprise, the results of the fertilizer-and-explosives attack on the Oklahoma clouds by the Bureau of Reclamation were described as "inconclusive," in keeping with the tradition of its experiments. This is not to say that nothing happened, however.

"I will admit," wryly observed Ferdie Deering, "that this operation produced downpours on or about September 4, 1971, that made farmers in Tillman and adjacent counties eligible for flood relief at the same time they were eligible for drought relief."

In the spring of 1972 Krick at last was called into action, and by that autumn he was operating all nine of Oklahoma's cloud-seeding programs, covering more than seven million acres—and it was raining. Within months both of Lawton's city reservoirs were brimming for the first time in recent memory. "Every area that has a cloud-seeding program has received more rain than the surrounding area," Ferdie Deering told Governor Hall.

It was raining so much that when it got to be above normal in the fall—140 percent in one locality—all but two of Krick's seeding operations were shut down until next year's wheat harvest was over.

But the drought of 1971 had cost Oklahoma $250 million of its crops, and farmers and businessmen went ahead on their own to get Krick's ground-based cloud-seeding projects set up over a larger portion of the state on a permanent basis. The generators would be turned on as needed and as Krick, by his long-range forecasting, saw the proper seeding conditions developing.

But now a threat to these do-it-yourself plans appeared from a new quarter of the United States government. "Another federal bureau which for many years openly opposed efforts to increase rainfall has now entered the picture and is looking at Oklahoma," reported the *Oklahoma City Times*. "Formerly called the U.S.

Weather Bureau, it now uses the more distinguished title of National Oceanic and Atmospheric Administration (NOAA)."

Eugene Bollay, one of Krick's students in 1935 and now head of NOAA's weather experiments in Boulder, Colorado, was in town, the *Times* noted, and in a conference with the state's own Weather Study Modification Study Committee, told the members he was running a study to find a good place on the Great Plains to make a ten-year study of cloud-seeding. The study just to find the place to make the study was expected to cost $100,000.

The right place, as Bollay saw it, appeared to be the western third of Oklahoma. This meant that whatever the natives were doing to bring more rain to this vast region would have to stop, again to preserve the purity of the government's work.

"It is not likely," observed the *Times* with understatement, "that many folks in western Oklahoma would agree to shut down productive cloud-seeding efforts in order to provide scientists with a drought laboratory for the next ten years."

The newspaper quickly proved correct on this score. With a storm of protest rising, the government took steps to conquer by division.

"Bureaucrats from Denver and other places, aided by personnel from the University of Oklahoma, are holding meetings to try to persuade Oklahoma to abandon interest in a dozen locally-controlled cloud-seeding projects that brought them rain last summer when it was badly needed," Ferdie Deering wrote in May, 1973. "They are particularly burned up because Krick's contract projects in Oklahoma are succeeding. They do not want local people telling them whether to seed or not to seed, or to have other authority."

As the Oklahomans held out against the government's plan to take away a third of the state for its experiments, the Bureau of Reclamation announced a compromise scheme, grandiosely called "A Conceptual Plan For a High Plains Cooperative Program." The new plan would take not a third of the state but *all* of it—but allowed private operators to work with them. (What this would do

146

to the chastity of the government's findings wasn't brought out.) Priced at $20 million, the plan covered not only Oklahoma but large areas of seven other states as well—"continuing and repeating research that the Bureau has been doing since 1961," Ferdie Deering observed sourly.

It looked as if it would still be quite a while before there was any rain with a helping hand from the government. The timetable called for the "studies" to begin in 1975, the first report in 1980, and maybe some operational seeding by 1990.

However, since private lands were involved, the government needed the owners' permission before it could proceed. Nothing came of "A Conceptual Plan For a High Plain Cooperative Program" in Oklahoma, but it went ahead in Kansas, Texas and Montana. As spreading disaster bore out Krick's forecast of years before—WESTERN DROUGHT DEEPENS, MIDWEST DROUGHT LOSSES MOUNTING, NEW ENGLAND DROUGHT WORST IN 27 YEARS, DUST STORM MOVES INTO SOUTHEAST—and the United States Government went on "researching" what to do about it, Irving Krick was a busy man.

14

They're Beginning To Listen

Paul Caubin, vice-president of the Krick organization, took the call. It came from a farmer in southwest Louisiana who remembered Krick's work in those parts during the fifties, including filling the reservoirs for the city of Shreveport and who, himself, had remained a client until five years before.

"We haven't had any rain around here for a month," the caller said plaintively. "If we don't get some real soon, there go our cotton and soybeans. Do you think you could help us?"

"It's a little late, but we'll see what we can do," Caubin answered.

"We're having a meeting tonight to decide what to do. How soon could you get down here and get working?"

In less than twenty-four hours Caubin himself was on the scene, taking personal charge for an old client. In a short time the cloud-seeding generators were shipped in by air and placed about the hills and fields, ready to start spouting silver iodide crystals into the reluctant sky.

The Louisiana project was no sooner underway than there came a call from a group of wheat farmers in Alberta, Canada, who were

outside the area where cloud-seeding experiments were being conducted by the provincial government. Krick had worked with them
before, from 1956 to 1968, with well remembered results. The
rainfall increased markedly, and the hail, scourge of their crops
for as as long as any could remember, decreased by about 70 percent.

By the growers' own computations, the benefits added up to a
gain of between $4000 and $6000 more income per section than
in any other area of Alberta.

"We want you back," Jim Bishop, head of the Alberta Weather
Modification Co-op, said to Krick.

With seeding projects going in Michigan, Texas, Minnesota,
Louisiana and Oklahoma (as of 1977 Krick held all current permits
for cloud-seeding in the Sooner State), he was about out of generators, but he was able to accommodate his old friends in Canada.

At about the same time, some farmers in south central Minnesota asked him to turn off his generators temporarily. The rains had
brought them the prospect of the best corn crop in years, and they
needed a few sunny days to get the hay in.

"It does seem that we have effectively increased much needed
rainfall," gratefully wrote Pat DuBois, President of Central Minnesota Weather, Inc., at Sauk Centre.

For any location where seeding is to be done, the generator network is first established on a map, according to the prevailing
weather patterns of the region. The generators may be spaced fifty
or sixty miles from the target area. For a project for Menomenee
County, Michigan, for example, the generators are spotted primarily
over in Wisconsin.

They are maintained and turned on and off by people hired
locally—service station operators, farmers, high school boys—one
man for each generator. The tenders are directed by controllers in
Palm Springs, kept abreast of shifting weather behavior in the area
by 1200-word-a-minute teletype connected to the government's facilities at Suitland, Maryland, clearinghouse for weather throughout
the world.

150

"We only have a half dozen key men, but in a way we have thousands of people keyed to our operations," Krick said, "because every weather observer in every country on earth is really working with us. We get the information over all the government teletype circuits, the facsimile circuits, the satellite data—everything we need. That's the one thing the Weather Bureau has that we appreciate and is superior—the observation, collection, and dissemination of information."

Current winds, temperature, and humidity readings are used by the controllers to determine what's happening to the silver iodide as the plumes from each generator stream upward, including how fast it's rising. It's a precision operation all the way.

"Critics say they don't know where the stuff's going," Krick said exasperatedly. "Well, they don't—but we do!"

The controller is frequently George Orlich, a onetime Air Force meteorologist, who was with Krick in London on D-Day. As Orlich telephones the operators around the country and Canada to tell them when to turn their generators on or off as the case may be, and for how long, he identifies himself by code, so that the operators can be sure they're talking to him. Probably, however, they know his voice, for the chances are he is the man who placed the generators and hired them. But the code identification takes care of those fun-loving fellows who will call an operator and say, "Turn on your generator."

As a further precaution, a monitor tours the network of generators at every project, seeing to it that the operators are on the job and the equipment maintained.

The chief work of the day at Krick's headquarters is long-range forecasting, the organization's specialty. An oil company with heating oil to sell wants to know what the temperatures are going to be in all the eastern states each month from November to April. Another oil firm with tankers at sea asks about the weather outlook for the next seven days each Friday during the hurricane season— or every three hours if there is a hurricane in the making.

A farmer with 1000 acres ready for planting in the Colorado River valley needs to know, no later than tomorrow, if there is going to be any frost before December 1. If so, he'll plant maize. If not, it will be cotton, which pays more.

A utility company in the East wants Krick's weather projections for years in the future—for 1981 and 1982. This will help them decide what capital investment is necessary to meet the power loads they may be faced with by that time.

A company that builds oil refineries, barging giant modules to Alaska to put up a $700 million refinery, wants the sea and swell forecasts from Seattle to Alaska to insure that they didn't get swamped by high seas at the piers as they unloaded. This was what Krick had done for General Patton during the war. Not a module was lost.

Cattle feeders ask if the commodity market is going up or down, so they'll know the best time to stock up on feed. A broker writes in wanting to know about the wheat harvest in Texas, or the cotton crop in the Delta—how many bushels per acre, whether above or below last year, and how much above or below the historical average. A cotton grower asks how it looks for the competition in California, the Delta, eastern Arizona—in distant Turkey.

From overseas a fruit shipper in Greece, wondering whether to ship in heated or unheated cars, asks what the temperatures are going to be en route to—say—Bulgaria and Poland next winter. An umbrella manufacturer in West Germany wants the rain forecast for all next year for the whole of Europe. How much rain is there going to be where and when? He can then estimate how many umbrellas to make and know where to send them.

Southern Spain, where Krick worked in the fifties, is heard from with a request from vegetable and citrus growers for the rainfall and temperature figures for each month of the coming year. They raise crops all year, but there is frost to worry about.

There are less weighty queries. A man phoned from Buffalo, New York, asking what kind of day it was going to be for his daughter's

152

wedding. "A friend of mine got forecasts from you for both his daughters' weddings," he explained.

As the questions come in regarding the most asked about topic in the world—the weather—Krick continues to improve his resources for answering them. "We are preparing to update our data base and extend our projections out into the twenty-first century," he says, referring to the data bank which currently enables them to make detailed, day-to-day forecasts for much of the Northern Hemisphere through 1985.

"Then we can give water management people here in the West a detailed and complete picture year to year of what the water resources will be for a twenty-year interval," he said. "This will allow them to plan and operate water projects much more effectively than anything that's been possible in the past."

The first step is the forecast. "This is fundamental to anything that eventually is done to modify the weather on a regional basis," Krick explained. "If you know what the upcoming weather regime is going to be, you set your priorities to take maximum advantage of what's coming, handling flood control properly in excess rainfall years and storage properly in the dry years."

If you ask Krick, there was no excuse for the water shortage in California in 1977, despite the state's worst drought in history, with water rationed and reservoirs getting so low by midsummer that soon there wouldn't be enough "head" to turn the generators of the power companies.

The Golden State's water famine could have been prevented, Krick declared, by seeding all river basins along the Sierras and the Upper Colorado River Basin to increase the snowpack, as he wanted to do when he moved to Denver in 1951, at the invitation of Governor Dan Thornton and the Denver Water Board. Nothing came of the plan because Congress failed to pass legislation, introduced by Senator Dominick, that would have provided money for the project.

"The annual flow of the Colorado could be increased by at least two million acre-feet a year," Krick maintained flatly. "Stored at Lake Powell and Lake Mead in surplus years, this would help meet any contingency during droughts such as that now being experienced in California. Thus, there is no excuse in 1977 for water curtailment in the state." Seeding the Columbia River Basin when appropriate would also alleviate power shortages in California.

Even for day to day operations, seeding to increase rain or snow must be done in advance, Krick stressed. "The whole air stream ahead of the weather front—maybe hundreds of cubic miles—is infused with silver iodide crystals, ready to go to work when the front arrives."

It's no good waiting until a likely looking cloud comes along and then rushing aloft with an airplane and squirting it with silver iodide from wing mounts. "Cloud-chasing," Krick scornfully calls it—and "primitive," tried and discarded as ineffective for broad-scale work by him and his associates a generation ago.

At best, this frenetic procedure may bring down 5 or 10 percent more water than would have fallen on its own. Or it may stop rain altogether from overseeding.

By the use of ground generators, in contrast to aircraft, Krick routinely doubles a snowfall and increases the rain from an individual storm by several hundred percent—up to 50 percent of historical averages for the year, he maintains.

Yet the outfit with the airplane, still favored by the government after thirty years of experimentation, often wins the competition with Krick for a seeding project. "Guys with planes have radar and sophisticated equipment of all kinds. All we have is just these little boxes sitting around controlled from our weather central in Palm Springs. You don't see or hear anything—no whistles, no rockets shooting off-nothing. We lost three jobs that way this year."

The man responsible for keeping the day by day prognostic charts, or weather maps of the future, about five years out in front, is Newton Stone, who came to Krick as a student in the old CalTech days and stayed on to become a professor. Stone first visited MIT with the idea of attending, but decided to go to CalTech out of curiosity after the MIT people spoke belittlingly of Krick and his ideas.

To arrive at his product, Stone juggles a bewildering montage of maps, charts and computerized esoterica, so complex that a new man needs at least a year and a half of concentrated study even to attempt the work under supervision. Moreover, he must be a meteorologist to begin with—a forecaster who agrees that the atmosphere is all one piece, functioning as such. Only about one in fifty applicants qualifies to work for Krick.

"We are a small group of dedicated, determined scientists and engineers who had an idea forty years ago which we felt it was important to develop for society," Krick said. "We were encouraged by Robert Millikan and we stayed together, never departing from our objective. The key to our success is being closely knit, knowing what we wanted, and sticking with it."

The secrets of the methods and techniques they worked out through the years—and continue to refine—Krick selectively shares with other private forecasters, so that, as he says, "they can function effectively. Maybe among us all we can counteract the various advisory groups we have had to contend with over the years."

Additionally, Krick is augmenting the old guard with new men whom he personally plans to train. "I'm going to take them right from scratch and put them through our methods," he said. "I'll make them draw prognostic charts and draw wave form analysis and all the rest of it."

The schoolroom will be the spacious marble-floored living room of Krick's Moorish style mansion at the upper end of Palm Springs, under the 10,000-foot peak of Mount San Jacinto. "We'll have a slide projector and screen right here—after working hours. They'll go through this just like a student and I'll tell them you're not earning your salt until you know our method and we're all on the same wavelength."

Expanding his staff may be timely for Krick. "I've been talking for twenty years," he complained one day in 1977 as the California drought was hurting more and more, "but nobody listens."

Not long afterward, a state water official discovered that of the five forecasts the state had paid for, including that of the former long-range expert for the Weather Bureau, Krick's was the only one that hit the mark: 1976–77 was going to be the driest year on record. The man from the state who revealed Krick's bull's-eye prediction was none other than Don Robie, director of California's Department of Water Resources, who told about it at a meeting of the California Water Commission. The story made page 1 of the Sacramento *Bee* on July 6, 1977.

Bureaucracy seemed finally to be bending an ear toward Irving Krick. At least that was the way it looked in California, where stream-flows were down to a trickle, reservoirs were drying up, and the loss to farmers and cattlemen alone, officials estimated, stood at $1 billion.

In Washington, though, action followed more nostalgic lines. Hearings were scheduled to begin on legislation calling for research to find out how to forecast the weather. The outlay this time: around $150 million.

Index

158

The Author

Victor Boesen is the author of the well-received *Doing Something About the Weather* from Putnam's. A free lance who has published many books and written articles for national magazines, he lives with his wife in Pacific Palisades, California.